6

Show What You Know® on the COMMON CORE

Assessing Student Knowledge of the Common Core State Standards (CCSS)

Mathematics

Published by:

Show What You Know® Publishing
www.showwhatyouknowpublishing.com

Distributed by:
Lorenz Educational Press, a Lorenz company
P.O. Box 802
Dayton, OH 45401-0802
www.LorenzEducationalPress.com

Standards are from the Common Core State Standards Initiative Web site at www.corestandards.org dated 2011.

Printed in the United States of America

ISBN: 978-1-5923-0459-2

Acknowledgements

Show What You Know® Publishing acknowledges the following for their efforts in making this assessment material available for students, parents, and teachers:

Cindi Englefield, President/Publisher
Eloise Boehm-Sasala, Vice President/Managing Editor
Jennifer Harney, Editor/Illustrator

About the Contributors

The content of this book was written BY teachers FOR teachers and students and was designed specifically for the Common Core State Standards for Grade 6 Mathematics. Contributions to the Mathematics section of this book were also made by the educational publishing staff at Show What You Know® Publishing. Dr. Jolie S. Brams, a clinical child and family psychologist, is the contributing author of the Test Anxiety and Test-Taking Strategies chapters of this book. Without the contributions of these people, this book would not be possible.

Table of Contents

Introduction

Under the leadership of the National Governors Association (NGA) and the Council of Chief State School Officers (CCSSO), forty-eight states, two territories, and the District of Columbia joined the Common Core State Standards Initiative (CCSS) in 2009.

The CCSS has produced Common Core State Standards to provide uniformity and high standards for student achievement in grades K–12 across the nation. These core standards provide a consistent, clear understanding of what students are expected to learn, so teachers and parents have a roadmap for what they need to do to help them. Further, these standards provide appropriate benchmarks for all students, regardless of where they live, and allow states to more effectively help all students to succeed.

To develop these standards, CCSSO and the NGA worked with representatives from participating states, a wide range of educators, content experts, researchers, national organizations, and community groups. The adopted core standards reflect the invaluable feedback from the general public, teachers, parents, business leaders, states, and content area experts.

As reflected in our Show What You Know® on the Common Core Student Workbooks and Parent/Teacher Editions for grades 3–8, Reading and Mathematics are the first subjects chosen for the Common Core State Standards because these two subjects are skills, upon which students build skill sets in other subject areas. They are also the subjects most frequently assessed for accountability purposes.

The Show What You Know® on the Common Core series for grades 3–8 is designed to review the new core standards and identify areas of students' strengths and needed improvement through diagnostic tests aligned to the core standards. In addition, the series provides chapters on test anxiety, test-taking strategies, and glossaries of terms for Reading and Mathematics to help prepare students with the knowledge and skills they need to succeed in the future.

Common Core State Standards will help ensure that students are receiving a high-quality education consistently, from school to school and state to state. These standards are a first step—a key building block—in providing students with a high-quality education that will prepare them for success in college and careers.

About the Show What You Know® Program

Show What You Know® Publishing has been developing test-preparation products since 1993. These products teach test-taking skills that are specific to state assessments and provide students with practice on full-length tests that simulate the format of state assessments. We understand that many students are not good test takers because they get nervous and may experience test anxiety. To help students with this issue, we provide a chapter, written by a child psychologist, that explains what test anxiety is, what it feels like, and ways to reduce the anxiety before, during, and after testing. Research has proven that three elements must exist for test success: knowledge, test-taking skills, and confidence. The Show What You Know® test-preparation program helps to ensure test success.

How to Use This Program

There are numerous ways to use the Student Workbook and Parent/Teacher Edition to help prepare your students for the Mathematics assessment. But before your students begin the assessments, take time to review the Test Anxiety and Test-Taking Strategies chapters in the Student Workbook to help them learn how to be better test takers. These important concepts can really improve students' test scores—it works!

Tips to Reduce Test Anxiety

You can read the entire chapter on test anxiety in the Student Workbook, or you can break it up into different sections, allowing yourself plenty of time to discuss and practice the methods suggested to reduce test stress. Identify what test anxiety is, and help students learn the symptoms. Explain to them that test anxiety is normal, and that there are ways it can be overcome. Tell them how being a little nervous will motivate them to do their best, but being very nervous could make them forget information they need to know for the test.

The rest of the Test Anxiety chapter offers activities to show ways to overcome test stress, such as thinking positively instead of negatively, emphasizing the importance of good physical health, and studying and practicing for the test. These are skills that will help your students succeed on state assessments, as well as other tests your students will face throughout their lives.

Test-Taking Strategies That Work!

The Test-Taking Strategies chapter can be used in a class discussion. The chapter gives specific test-taking strategies for state assessments. After reviewing the chapter, ask students if they have found ways to help them prepare for tests. Maybe they like to read stories with their parents or they make sure to get extra sleep the week of a test. All of these strategies can be used to help them do well on state assessments and other tests.

The Purpose of the Assessments

After you have walked your students through the Test Anxiety and Test-Taking Strategies chapters, students can take two, 40-question assessments for Mathemataics.

These tests were designed to simulate state assessments so that students can become familiar with the actual look of the test. The more familiar students are with the look of the test, the more confidence they will have when they take the actual assessment.

Correlation Charts Track Students' Strengths and Weaknesses

In this Parent/Teacher Edition, there are Correlation Charts for each Assessment. The standards as well as test item answers are listed for each question. To use the chart, write the students' names in the left-hand column. When students miss a question, place an "X" in the corresponding box. A column with a large number of "Xs" shows that your class needs more practice with that particular standard. You can quickly identify the needs of individual students.

Answer Key with Sample Responses

Answers to the Mathematics assessments are provided in the Parent/Teacher Edition. The correct answer is given, and for short-answer questions, a sample response is offered.

Skills Chart

A skills chart for each assessment is provided in the Parent/Teacher Edition. The chart serves as a mini directory identifying the Common Core State Standard used for each assessment question, the correct answer choice, and the keyword(s) which summarize(s) the standard.

Additional Teaching Tools

A glossary of mathematics terms is provided in the Student Workbook to help your students understand terms that they should be familiar with in the sixth grade.

Suggested Timeline for Program Use

Now that you have a better understanding of how to use the Show What You Know® Test-Preparation Program, here is a suggested timeline for you to use to incorporate the program into your teaching schedule:

Suggested Timeline for Using the Show What You Know® on the Common Core for Grade 6 Mathematics, Student Workbook	
Week 1	Test Anxiety chapter
Week 2	Test-Taking Strategies chapter
Week 3	Review Glossary of Terms and Illustrations for Mathematics
Week 4	Mathematics Assessment One
Week 5	Additional Review After Results of Mathematics Assessment One
Week 6	Mathematics Assessment Two

Thank you for implementing the Show What You Know® Test-Preparation Program in your classroom. Good luck to you and all of your students as they prepare for their state assessment!

Test Anxiety

Introduction

The contents of the Test Anxiety chapter, from the *Show What You Know® on the Common Core for Grade 6 Mathematics, Student Workbook*, begin on the next page. This chapter will help students begin to understand why they may feel some anxiety before taking a test. This anxiety is normal and is experienced by many people, not only students. The chapter offers information on different types of test takers and ideas on how to reduce worrisome feelings about tests.

Test Anxiety

What is Test Anxiety?

Test anxiety is just a fancy name for feeling nervous about tests. Everyone knows what it is like to be nervous. Feeling nervous is not a good experience.

Many students have anxiety about taking tests, so if you are a test worrier, don't let it worry you. Most likely, many of your fellow students and friends also have fearful feelings about tests but do not share these feelings with others. Sixth grade is a time when everyone wants to seem "grown up," and few sixth graders want to look weak or afraid in the eyes of their friends or their teachers. But not talking to others about anxiety only makes the situation worse. It makes you feel alone and also makes you wonder if there is something "wrong" with you. Be brave! Talk to your friends and teachers about test anxiety. You will feel better for sharing.

What Does It Feel Like to Have Test Anxiety?

Students who have test anxiety don't always feel the same way, but they always feel bad. Here are some ways that students feel when they are anxious about tests.

- **Students who have test anxiety rarely think good things about themselves.**
  They lack confidence in their abilities, and they are convinced they will do poorly on tests. Not only do they feel bad about themselves and their abilities, but they just can't keep negative thoughts out of their minds. They would probably make terrible detectives, because in spite of all the good things they could find out about themselves, they only think about what they can't do. And that's not the worst of it. Students with test anxiety also exaggerate. When they think of the smallest problem, it becomes a hundred times bigger, especially when they think about tests. They are very unforgiving of themselves. If they make a mistake, they always think the worst or exaggerate the situation. If they do poorly on a quiz, they never say, "Well, it's just a quiz, and I'll try better next time." Instead they think, "That test was terrible and I can only imagine how badly I'll do next week." For students with test anxiety, there is never a brighter day ahead. They don't think many good thoughts about themselves, and they certainly don't have a happy outlook on their lives.

- **Students who have test anxiety have poor "thinking habits."**
  Negative thinking is a habit just like any other habit. Some habits are good and some habits are bad, but negative thinking is probably the worst habit of all. A habit forms when you do something over and over again until it becomes so much a part of you that you don't think about it anymore. Students with test anxiety get into bad thinking habits. They develop negative ways of thinking about themselves and about schoolwork, especially about tests. They tend to make the worst out of situations and imagine all kinds of possibilities that probably will not happen. Their thoughts grow like a mushroom out of control. Besides having negative ideas about tests, they begin to have negative ideas about almost everything else in their lives. This is not a good way of thinking because the more negative they feel about themselves, the worse they do in school, and bad grades make them feel even worse about themselves. What a mess. Students who have constant negative thoughts about themselves and schoolwork probably have test anxiety.

- **Students who have test anxiety may feel physically uncomfortable or even ill.**
  It is important to know that your mind and body are connected. What goes on in your mind can change how your body feels, and how your body feels can influence what goes on in your thinking. When students have test anxiety, their thoughts might cause them to have physical symptoms which include a fast heartbeat, butterflies in the stomach, headaches, and all sorts of other physical problems. Some kids become so ill they end up going to the doctor because they believe they are truly sick. Some students miss a lot of school due to anxiety, but they aren't really ill. Instead, their thoughts are controlling their bodies in a negative way. Some anxious students do not realize that what they are feeling is anxiety. They miss many days of school, not because they are lazy or neglectful, but because they believe they truly are not feeling well. Unfortunately, the more school they miss, the more behind they are and the more nervous they feel. Students who suffer from test anxiety probably feel even worse on test days. Their uncomfortable physical feelings will make them either avoid the test completely or feel so bad during the test that they do poorly. Guess what happens then. They feel even worse about themselves, become more anxious, and the cycle goes on and on.

- **Students who have test anxiety "freak out" and want to escape.**
  Many students feel so bad when they are anxious that they will do anything to avoid that feeling. For most students, this means running away from problems, especially tests. Some students try to get away from tests by missing school. This does not solve any problems; the more a student is away from school, the harder schoolwork is, and the worse he or she feels. Some students worry about being worried. It may sound silly, but they are worried that they are going to freak out, and guess what happens . . . they do. They are so terrified that they will have uncontrollable anxious feelings that they actually get anxious feelings when thinking about this problem. For many students, anxiety is such a bad feeling that they will do anything not to feel anxious, even if it means failing tests or school. Although they know this will cause them problems in the future, their anxiety is so overwhelming they would rather avoid anxiety now and fail later. Unfortunately, this is usually what happens.

- **Students who have test anxiety do not show what they know on tests.**
  Students who have test anxiety do not make good decisions on tests. Instead of focusing their thoughts, planning out their answers, and using what they know, students find themselves "blanking out." They stare at the paper, and no answer is there. They become "stuck" and cannot move on. Some students come up with the wrong answers because their anxiety gets in the way of reading directions carefully and thinking about answers thoughtfully. Their minds are running in a hundred different ways and none of those ways seem to be getting them anywhere. They forget to use what they know, and they also forget to use study skills that can help students do their best. When students are so worried that they cannot make good decisions and use all of the talents they have, it is called test anxiety.

Are You One of These "Test-Anxious" Sixth Graders?

As you have seen, students with test anxiety have negative thoughts about themselves, often feel anxious to the point of being ill, freak out and want to escape, and rarely show what they know on tests. Do any of the following kids remind you of yourself?

Stay-Away Stephanie

Stephanie's thoughts tell her it is better to stay away from challenges, especially tests. Stephanie is a good girl, but she is always in trouble at school for avoiding tests. Sometimes, she really feels ill and begs her mom to allow her to stay home on test days. At other times, Stephanie does anything to avoid school, refusing to get up in the morning or to leave the house to catch the bus. Stephanie truly believes there is nothing worse than taking a test. She is so overwhelmed with anxiety that she forgets about the problems that will happen when she stays away from her responsibilities. Unfortunately, the more she stays away, the worse the situation becomes. Stay-Away Stephanie feels less nervous when she doesn't face a test, but she never learns to face her fears.

Worried Wendy

Wendy is the type of sixth grader who always expects the worst thing to happen. She has many negative thoughts. Even when situations have turned out to be OK, Wendy focuses on the few bad things that happened. She exaggerates negative events and forgets about everything good. Her mind races a mile a minute with all sorts of thoughts and ideas about tests. The more she thinks, the worse she feels, and her problems become unbelievably huge. Instead of just worrying about a couple of difficult questions on a test, she finds herself thinking about failing the whole test, being made fun of by her friends, being grounded by her parents, and never going to college. She completely forgets that her parents would never be so strict, that her friends like her for many more reasons than her test grades, and that she has all sorts of career choices ahead of her. No one is going to hold it against her if she performed poorly on a test. It is not going to ruin her life. However, Wendy believes all of that would happen. Her negative thoughts get in the way of thinking anything positive.

Critical Chris

Chris is the type of sixth grader who spends all of his time putting himself down. No matter what happens, he always feels he has been a failure. While some people hold grudges against others, Chris holds grudges against himself. No matter what little mistakes he makes, he can never forget them. Chris has had many good things happen to him in his life, and he has been successful many times. Unfortunately, Chris forgets all the good and only remembers the bad. Because he doesn't appreciate himself, Chris has test anxiety.

Victim Vince

Most sixth graders find it is important to take responsibility for their actions. It helps them understand that adulthood is just around the corner, and that they are smarter and more able than they ever thought they were. However, Vince is not like this. He can't take responsibility for himself at all. He thinks everything is someone else's fault and constantly complains about friends, parents, schoolwork, and especially tests. He tells himself, "They make those tests too hard." He sees the teachers as unfair, and he thinks life is generally against him. Vince does not feel there is anything he can do to help his situation, and there is little he thinks he can do to help himself with tests. Because he does not try to learn test-taking skills or to understand why he is afraid, he continues to feel hopeless and angry. Not surprisingly, he does poorly on tests, which only makes his thoughts about the world around him worse.

Perfect Pat

Everyone knows that there is more homework and responsibility in sixth grade than in previous grades. Everyone in the sixth grade needs to try his or her best, but no one should try as much as Pat does. All Pat does is worry. No matter what she does, it's never good enough. She will write book reports over and over and study for tests until she is exhausted. Trying hard is fine, but no matter what Pat does, she feels she has never done enough. Because she never accomplishes what she sets out to do (that would be impossible.), she worries all the time. Her anxiety level gets higher and higher. The more anxious she becomes, the worse she does on tests. This just makes her study and worry more. What a terrible situation!

How Do I Handle Test Anxiety?

Test anxiety is a very powerful feeling that convinces students they are weak and helpless. Feelings of test anxiety can be so powerful it seems there is nothing you can do to stop them. Anxiety seems to take over your mind and body and leaves you feeling like you are going to lose the test anxiety battle for sure.

The good news is that there are many simple things you can do to win the battle over test anxiety. If you can learn these skills in the sixth grade, you are on the road to success in school and for all other challenges in your life.

- **Change the way you think.**
  Most of us don't "think about how we think." We just go along thinking our thoughts and never really considering whether they are helpful or not helpful or if they are right or wrong. We rarely realize how much the way we think has to do with how well we get along in life. Our thoughts can influence how we feel about ourselves, how we get along with other people, how well we do in school, and how we perform on tests.
- **The Soda Pop Test.**
  Most sixth graders have heard a parent or teacher tell them, "There is more than one side to any story." One student reported that his grandfather used to say, "There's more than one way to paint a fence." Have you ever considered how you think about different situations? Most situations can be looked at in many ways, both good and bad.

  Take a can of soda pop and put it on your desk or dresser at home. Get out a piece of paper and a pen or a pencil. Now, draw a line down the middle of the paper. On one side, put a heading: "All the bad things about this can of soda pop." On the other side put another heading: "All the good things about this can of soda pop." If you think about that can of soda pop, you might come up with the following chart.

All the bad things about this can of soda pop	All the good things about this can of soda pop
Not an attractive color	Easy-to-read lettering
It's getting warm	Nice to have something to drink
Not much in the can	Inexpensive
Has a lot of sugar	Recyclable aluminum cans

Look how easy it is to write down good things or bad things about a silly can of soda pop. That can of soda pop is not really good or bad, it's just a can of soda pop, but we can either look at it in a positive way or we can think about everything negative that comes to our minds. Doesn't the same thing hold true for tests? Tests are not good or bad in themselves. Tests are just a way to challenge us and see what we know. Challenges can be stressful, but they can also be rewarding. Studying for tests can be boring and can take up a lot of free time, but we can also learn a lot and feel great about ourselves when we study. The way you think about tests will help determine how you do in a test-taking situation. Most importantly, how you feel about tests is related to your level of anxiety about test taking. Students who have negative thoughts and feelings about tests become anxious. Students who think positively are less anxious. To reduce test anxiety, try thinking about tests and testing situations using a positive frame of mind.

- **All or Nothing Thinking.**
  Nothing is ever as simple as it seems. Sometimes we convince ourselves something is going to be "awful" or "wonderful." Rarely does it turn out that way.

  Trouble comes along when students think tests are going to be an "awful" experience. If you dread something happening, it is only going to make things worse. Also, you may be wrong. Nothing is as terrible as it seems. All the negative thoughts you have about the upcoming test cannot possibly be true. Thinking something is "awful" or "terrible" and nothing else only leads to trouble and failure. The more negative you feel about something, the worse things turn out.

  Very few things are "all good" or "all bad." This is especially true for tests. Recognizing the "bad" parts of tests can help you be successful. For example, the fact that you need to study for tests, to pay attention while you are taking tests, and to understand there are probably many more fun things to do in school than take tests are all "true" thoughts. "Good" thoughts are just as true, including the good feelings one gets from studying and the chance that you might do well. Having "all or nothing" thinking is going to get you nowhere. Successful and happy students know some experiences are better than others, but they try to look at a situation from all sides.

- **Mind Reading.**
  Some students believe they can read the minds of their parents and teachers. They assume if they do poorly on a test, everyone will think they are "dumb" or "lazy." The more their minds create all the terrible things that people may say about them, the more anxious they get. This just increases anxiety and definitely does not help students do well on tests.

- **Catastrophizing.**
  When people catastrophize, they make everything a catastrophe. A catastrophe is a disaster. It is when something terrible happens. When a student catastrophizes, his or her mind goes on and on creating terrible scenes of disasters. If someone put all these ideas into a movie script, the writer might be rich.

  Your state proficiency test is an important part of a sixth-grader's school year. It is a test that helps the student, the teacher, and the school. However, a sixth-grade student is much more than just his or her score on the test. Each student is an individual who has his or her own great personality, talents, and other successes in school. If what people catastrophized about was really true, the whole world would be a terrible mess. Imagine if your mother cooked a dinner that didn't turn out quite right. This might mean everyone has to go out for fast food, but you wouldn't love your mother any less. It would be catastrophizing if your mother said, "Now that I burned the dinner, none of my kids will love me. They will probably just want to move out as quickly as they can, and my life will be ruined." Catastrophizing about a test is just as bad. Thinking that this test is going to be the worst experience of your life and that your future will be ruined will not help you feel comfortable when preparing for and taking the test.

- **Making "Should" Statements.**
  Students make themselves anxious when they think they "should" do everything. They feel they "should" be as smart as everyone else, "should" study more, and "should" not feel anxious about tests. All these thoughts are pretty ridiculous. You can't always be as smart as the next person, and you do not have to study until you drop to do well on tests. Instead of kicking yourself for not being perfect, it is better to think about all the good things you have done in your life. This will help you do better on tests and be happier in your life by reducing your anxiety.

How Do I Replace Worried Thoughts with Positive Ones?

As we have learned, there are all kinds of thoughts that make us anxious, such as feeling we "should" do everything, thinking we can read peoples' minds, catastrophizing, and thinking only bad thoughts about a situation. Learning how to stop these types of thoughts is very important. Understanding your thoughts and doing something about them help control test anxiety.

People who are worried or anxious can become happier when thinking positive thoughts. Even when situations are scary, such as a visit to the dentist, "positive imagery" is helpful. "Positive imagery" means thinking good thoughts to keep from thinking anxious thoughts. Positive and negative thoughts do not go together. If you are thinking something positive, it is almost impossible to think of something negative. Keep this in mind when test anxiety starts to become a bother.

Try these ideas the next time you find yourself becoming anxious.

- **Thoughts of Success.**
  Thinking "I can do it" thoughts can chase away thoughts of failure. Imagine times you were successful, such as when you performed well in a dance recital or figured out a complicated brain teaser. These are good things to think about. Telling yourself you have been successful in the past and can be successful in the future will chase away thoughts of anxiety.

- **Relaxing Thoughts.**
  Some people find that thinking calming or relaxing thoughts is helpful. Picturing a time in which you felt comfortable and happy can lessen your anxious feelings. Imagine yourself playing a baseball game, running through a park, or eating an ice cream cone; these are all positive thoughts that may get in the way of anxious ones. Some students find that listening to music on the morning of a test is helpful. It probably doesn't matter what music you listen to, as long as it makes you feel good about yourself, confident, and relaxed.

  Just as you can calm your mind, it is also important for you to relax your body. Practice relaxing your body. When students have test anxiety, their muscles become stiff. In fact, the whole body becomes tense. Taking deep breaths before a test and letting them out slowly as well as relaxing muscles in your body are all very helpful ways to feel less anxious. Your school counselors will probably have more ideas about relaxation. You may find that relaxation doesn't just help you on tests, but is helpful for other challenging situations and for feeling healthy overall.

- **Don't Let Yourself Feel Alone.**
  Everyone feels more anxious when they feel alone and separate from others. Talking to your friends, parents, and teachers about your feelings helps. Feeling anxious about tests does not mean there is something wrong with you. You will be surprised to find that many of your friends and fellow students also feel anxious about tests. You may be even more surprised to learn your parents and teachers have also had test anxiety. They know what you are going through and are there to support you.

- **Take Care of Yourself.**
  Everyone is busy. Many sixth graders are involved in all sorts of activities, including sports, music, and helping around the house. Often, you are so busy you forget to eat breakfast or you don't get enough sleep. Eating and sleeping right are important, especially before a test like your state proficiency test. If you are not a big breakfast eater, try to find something that you like to eat and get in the habit of eating breakfast. When you do not eat right, you may feel shaky and have a hard time concentrating, and your anxiety can increase. Being tired does not help either. Try to get in the habit of going to bed at a good time every night (especially the night before a test) so you can feel fresh, rested, and confident.

- **Practice Your Test-Taking Success.**
  People who have accomplished incredibly difficult goals have used their imaginations to help them achieve success. They thought about what they would do step by step to be successful.

  You can do the same. Think about yourself on the morning of the test. Imagine telling yourself positive thoughts and eating a good breakfast. Think about arriving at school and feeling confident that you will do fine on the test. Imagine closing your eyes before the test, breathing deeply, relaxing, and remembering all the study skills you have learned. The more you program your mind to think in a successful and positive way, the better off you will be.

- **Learn to Use Study Skills.**
  The next chapter in this book will help you learn test-taking strategies. The more you know about taking tests successfully, the calmer you will feel. Knowledge is power. Practice test-taking strategies to reduce your test anxiety.

- **Congratulate Yourself During the Test.**
  Instead of thinking, "I've only done five problems and I've got eight pages to go," or "I knew three answers were right but one mixed me up," reward yourself for what you have done. Tell yourself, "I got some answers right so far, so I bet I can do more." After all, if you don't compliment yourself, who will?

Conclusion

You are not alone if you feel stressed about tests. It is probably good to feel a little anxious, because it motivates you to do well. However, if you feel very anxious about tests, then reading, re-reading, and practicing the suggestions in this chapter will help you "tackle your test anxiety."

Test-Taking Strategies

Introduction

The contents of the Test-Taking Strategies chapter, from the *Show What You Know® on the Common Core for Grade 6 Mathematics, Student Workbook*, begin on the next page. This chapter will introduce students to test-taking strategies. These strategies are hints students can use for any test, but they are especially helpful for state assessments. This chapter will give students the tools they need to become successful test takers.

Test-Taking Strategies

All Students Can Do Their Best on Tests!

Most students want to do their best on tests. Tests are one important way for teachers to know how well students are doing and for students to understand how much progress they are making in their studies. Tests, like your state proficiency test, help schools measure how well students are learning so teachers and principals can make their schools even better. Students can do the best job possible in "showing what they know" by learning how to be good test takers.

It's just not possible to do a good job without the right tools. Test-taking strategies are tools to help you perform well on tests. Everyone needs good tools and strategies when facing a problem. If you do not have these, even the smartest or most talented person will do poorly. Think about people who are "wizards" at fixing cars and trucks. Your family's car "dies" in the middle of the road. The situation looks pretty hopeless. How are you ever going to get to that basketball game tomorrow if your parent's car is a mechanical mess? Suddenly, "magic" happens. The mechanic at the repair shop calls your parents and tells them the car is ready, just a day after it broke down. How did this happen? It happened because the auto-repair mechanic had a great deal of knowledge about cars. Most importantly, he had the right tools and strategies to fix the car. He knew how to look at the problem, and when he figured out what to do, he had some special gadgets to get the job done. You also can find special ways that will help you be a successful test taker.

Tools You Can Use on Tests Throughout Your Life!

Be An "Active Learner."
You can't learn anything by being a "sponge." Just because you are sitting in a pool of learning (your classroom) does not mean you are going to learn anything just by being there. Instead, students learn when they actively think and participate during the school day. Students who are active learners pay attention to what is being said. They also constantly ask themselves and their teachers questions about the subject. When able, they participate by making comments and joining discussions. Active learners enjoy school, learn more, feel good about themselves, and usually do better on tests. Remember the auto-repair mechanic? That person had a lot of knowledge about fixing cars. All the tools and strategies in the world will not help unless you have benefited from what your teachers have tried to share.

Being an active learner takes time and practice. If you are the type of student who is easily bored or frustrated, it is going to take some practice to use your classroom time differently. Ask yourself the following questions.

- Am I looking at the teacher?
- Do I pay attention to what is being said?
- Do I have any questions or ideas about what the teacher is saying?
- Do I listen to what my fellow students are saying and think about their ideas?
- Do I work with others to try to solve difficult problems?
- Do I look at the clock and wonder what time school will be over, or do I appreciate what is happening during the school day and how much I can learn?
- Do I try to think about how my schoolwork might be helpful to me now or in the future?

Although you do need special tools and strategies to do well on tests, the more you learn, the better chance you have of doing well on tests. Think about Kristen.

There was a young girl named Kristen,
Who was bored and wouldn't listen.
She didn't train
To use her smart brain
And never knew what she was missing!

Don't Depend on Luck.
Preparing for your state proficiency test might feel stressful or boring at times, but it is an important part of learning how to show what you know and doing your best. Even the smartest student needs to spend time taking practice tests and listening to the advice of teachers about how to do well. Luck alone is not going to help you do well on tests. People who depend on luck do not take responsibility for themselves. Some people who believe in luck do not want to take the time and effort to do well. It is easier for them to say, "It's not my fault I did poorly. It's just not my lucky day." Some people just do not feel very good about their abilities. They get in the habit of saying, "Whatever happens will happen." They believe they can never do well no matter how much they practice or prepare. Students who feel they have no control over what happens to them usually have poor grades and do not feel very good about themselves.

Your performance on tests is not going to be controlled by luck. Instead, you can have a lot of control over how well you do in many areas of your life, including test taking. Don't be like Chuck.

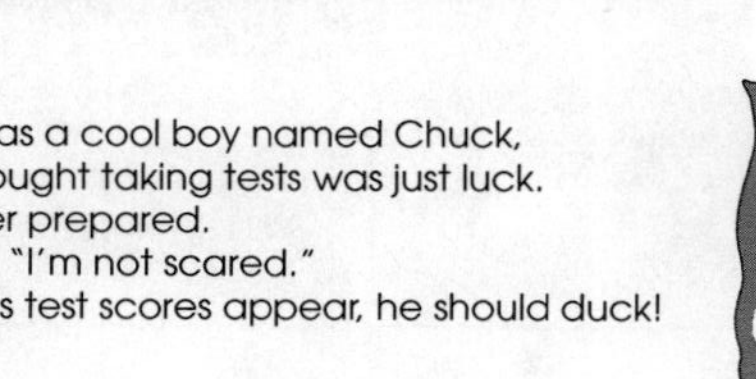

There was a cool boy named Chuck,
Who thought taking tests was just luck.
He never prepared.
He said, "I'm not scared."
When his test scores appear, he should duck!

Do Your Best Every Day.
Many students find sixth grade much different than other grades. Suddenly, the work seems really hard. Not only that, but your teachers are no longer treating you like a baby. That's good in some ways, because it gives you more freedom and responsibility, but there sure is a lot to learn. You might feel the same way about tests; you may feel you'll never be prepared. Many times when we are faced with new challenges, it is easy just to give up.

Students are surprised when they find that if they just set small goals for themselves, they can learn an amazing amount. If you learn just one new fact every day of the year, at the end of the year, you will know 365 new facts. You could use those to impress your friends and family. Now think about what would happen if you learned three new facts every day. At the end of the year, you would have learned 1,095 new facts. Soon you will be on your way to having a mind like an encyclopedia.

When you think about a test or any other academic challenge, try to focus on what you can learn step by step and day by day. You will be surprised how all of this learning adds up to make you one of the smartest sixth graders ever. Think about Ray.

There was a smart boy named Ray,
Who learned something new every day.
He was pretty impressed
With what his mind could possess.
His excellent scores were his pay!

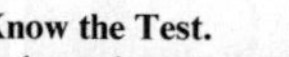

Get to Know the Test.
Most sixth graders are probably pretty used to riding in their parents' cars. They know how to make the air-conditioning cooler or warmer, how to change the radio stations, and how to adjust the volume on the radio. Think about being a passenger in a totally unfamiliar car. You might think, "What are all those buttons? How do I even turn on the air conditioner? How do I make the window go up and down?" Now, think about taking your state proficiency test. Your state proficiency test is a test, but it may be different than some tests you have taken in the past. The more familiar you are with the types of questions on the test and how to record your answers, the better you will do. Working through the Mathematics chapters in this book will help you get to know the test. Becoming familiar with the test is a great test-taking tool. Think about Sue.

There was a kid named Sue,
Who thought her test looked new.
"I never saw this before!
How'd I get a bad score?"
If she practiced, she might have a clue!

Read Directions and Questions Carefully!
One of the worst mistakes a student can make on a test is to ignore directions or to read questions carelessly. By the time some students are in the sixth grade, they think they have heard every direction or question ever invented, and it is easy for them to "tune out" directions. Telling yourself, "These directions are just like other directions," or "I'm not really going to take time to read this question because I know what the question will be," are not good test-taking strategies. It is impossible to do well on any test without knowing what is being asked.

Reading directions and questions slowly, repeating them to yourself, and asking yourself if what you are reading makes sense are powerful test-taking strategies. Think about Fred.

There was a nice boy named Fred,
Who ignored almost all that he read.
The directions were easy,
But he said, "I don't need these!"
He should have read them instead.

Know How to Fill in Those Answer Bubbles!
Most sixth graders have taken tests that ask them to fill in answer bubbles. You might be a very bright sixth grader, but you will never "show what you know" unless you fill in the answer bubbles correctly. Don't forget: a computer will be "reading" your multiple-choice question answers. If you do not fill in the answer bubble darkly or if you use a check mark or dot instead of a dark mark, your smart thinking will not be counted. Look at the examples given below.

Correct ● ● ● ● ●
Incorrect

Practice Here
○ ○ ○ ○
○ ○ ○ ○
○ ○ ○ ○

Test-Taking Strategies Show What You Know® on the Common Core for Grade 6 Mathematics

Learning how to fill in answer bubbles takes practice, practice, and more practice. It may not be how you are used to answering multiple-choice questions, but it is the only way to give a right answer on your state proficiency test. Think about Kay!

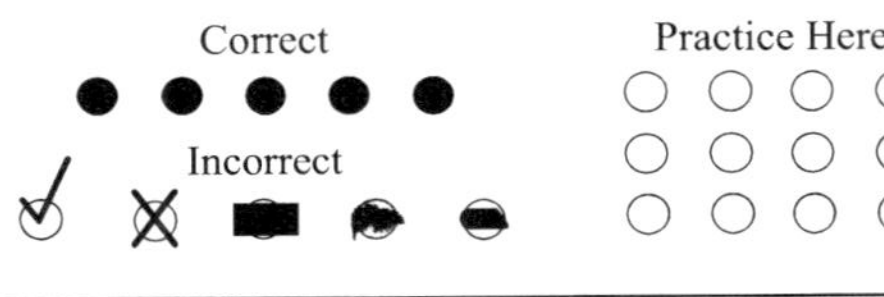

A stubborn girl named Kay,
Liked to answer questions her own way.
So her marked answer bubbles,
Gave her all sorts of troubles.
Her test scores ruined her day!

Speeding Through the Test Doesn't Help.
Most students have more than enough time to read and answer all the questions on a test. There will always be some students who finish the test more quickly than others, but this does not mean the test was easier for them or their answers are correct. Whether you finish at a faster rate or at a slower rate than other students in your class is not important. As long as you take your time, are well prepared, concentrate on the test, and use some of the skills in this book, you should be able to do just fine. You will not get a better score just because you finish the test before everyone else. Speeding through a test item or through a whole test does not help you do well. In fact, students do their best when they work at a medium rate of speed, not too slow and not too fast. Students who work too slowly tend to get worried about their answers and sometimes change correct answers into incorrect ones. Students who work too fast often make careless mistakes, and many of them do not read directions or questions carefully. Think about Liz.

There was a sixth grader named Liz,
Who sped through her test like a whiz.
She thought she should race
At a very fast pace,
But it caused her to mess up her quiz.

Answer Every Question.
There is no reason that you should not attempt to answer every question you encounter on a test. Even if you don't know the answer, there are ways for you to increase your chances of choosing the correct response. Use the helpful strategies described below to help you answer every question to the best of your ability.

- **If you don't know the answer, guess.**
  Did you know that on your state proficiency there is no penalty for guessing? That is really good news. That means you have a one out of four chance of getting a multiple-choice question right, even if you just close your eyes and guess. That means that for every four questions you guess, you should get about 25% (1 out of 4) of the questions right. Guessing alone is not going to make you a star on the test, but leaving multiple-choice items blank is not going to help you either.

  Now comes the exciting part. If you can rule out one of the four answer choices, your chances of answering correctly are now one out of three. You can almost see your test score improving right before your eyes.

  Although it is always better to be prepared for the test and to study in school, we all have to guess at one time or another. Some of us do not like to guess because we are afraid of choosing the wrong answer, but on a test, it is better to guess than leave an answer blank. Think about Jess.

There was a smart girl named Jess,
Who thought it was useless to guess.
If a question was tough,
She just gave up.
This only added to her stress.

- **Use a "code" to help you make good guesses.**
  Some students use a "code" to rate each answer when they feel they might have to guess. Using your pencil in the test booklet, you can mark the following codes next to each multiple-choice response so you can make the best possible guess. The codes are as follows:

(+) Putting a "plus sign" by your answer means you are not sure if this answer is correct, but you think this answer is probably more correct than the others.

(?) Putting a "question mark" by your answer means you are unsure if this is the correct answer, but you don't want to rule it out completely.

(–) Putting a "minus sign" by your answer means you are pretty sure this is the wrong answer. You should then choose from the other answers to make an educated guess.

Remember, it is fine to write in your test booklet. Think about Dwight.

There was a smart kid named Dwight,
Who marked answers that looked to be right.
He'd put a plus sign
Or a dash or a line.
Now the whole world knows he is bright!

- **Use what you know to "power guess."**
  Not everything you know was learned in a classroom. Part of what you know comes from just living your life. When you take a test, you should use everything you have learned in school, but you should also use your experiences outside the classroom to help you answer questions correctly. Using your "common sense," as well as other information you know, will help you do especially well on a test. Try to use what you know from the world around you to eliminate obviously wrong answers. If you can rule out just one answer that you are certain is not correct, you are going to greatly increase your chances of guessing another answer correctly. For example, if you are given a question in which you are asked to find the square footage of a home, and one of the answers seems very small, you might be able to count that answer out using your own experiences. Although the mathematics might be difficult for you, your common sense has eliminated one likely wrong answer. Think about Drew.

There was a boy named Drew,
Who forgot to use what he knew.
He had lots of knowledge.
He could have been in college!
But his right answers were few.

- **Do Not Get Stuck on One Question.**
  One of the worst things you can do on a test is to get stuck on one question. Your state proficiency test gives you many chances to show all that you have learned. Not knowing the answer to one or two questions is not going to hurt your test results very much.

  When you become stuck on a question, your mind plays tricks on you. You begin to think that you are a total failure, and your worries become greater and greater. This worrying gets in the way of your doing well on the rest of the test. Remember, very few students know all the answers on a test. If you are not sure of the answer after spending some time on it, mark it in your test booklet and come back to it later. When you to come back to that question later, you might find a new way of thinking. Sometimes, another question or answer later in the test will remind you of a possible answer to the question that had seemed difficult. If not, you can use your guessing strategies to solve the questions you are unsure of after you have answered all the questions you know. Also, when you move on from a troubling question and find you are able to answer other questions correctly, you will feel much better about yourself and you will feel calmer. This will help you have a better chance of succeeding on a question that made you feel "stuck." Think about Von.

There was a sweet girl named Von,
Who got stuck and just couldn't go on.
She'd sit there and stare,
But the answer wasn't there.
Before she knew it, all the time was gone.

- **Always, and This Means Always, Recheck Your Work.**
  Everyone makes mistakes. People make the most mistakes when they feel a little worried or rushed. Checking your work is a very important part of doing your best. This is particularly true in the Mathematics section, where careless mistakes can lead to a wrong answer, even when the student used the right steps. Going back and rechecking your work is very important. You can read a paragraph over again if there is something you do not understand or something that you forgot. In the Mathematics section, look at your calculations to make sure that you did not mistake one number for another and that you lined up your calculations neatly and legibly. If any numbers seem messy or unreadable, you might want to recheck your calculations. If an answer does not seem to make sense, go back and reread the question, or recheck your work. Think about Jen.

There was a quick girl named Jen,
Who read stuff once and never again.
It would have been nice
If she'd reread it twice.
Her test scores would be better then!

- **Pay Attention to Yourself and Not Others.**
  It is easy to look around the room and wonder how friends are doing. However, it is important to think about how you are using tools and strategies. Don't become distracted by friends. You are going to waste a lot of time if you try to figure out what your friends are doing. Instead, use that time to "show what you know."

  If it becomes hard for you to pay attention, give yourself a little break. If you feel you are getting a little tense or worried, or if a question seems tough, close your eyes for a second or two. Think positive thoughts. Try to put negative thoughts out of your mind. You might want to stretch your arms or feet or move around a little to help you focus. Anything you may do to help pay better attention to the test is a great test-taking strategy. Think about Kirk.

There was a boy named Kirk,
Who thought of everything but his work.
He stared into the air
And squirmed in his chair.
When his test scores come, he won't look!

General Test-Taking Strategies for Mathematics

The Mathematics Assessment will likely ask you to answer multiple-choice questions and short-answer questions. Here are some good strategies to use on the Mathematics Assessment.

- **Neatness Counts.**

  Numbers that no one can read, or that are out of place, may hurt your score. For short-answer questions and completion items, write your answer clearly in the space provided. For multiple-choice answers, make sure you fill in the answer circle completely.

- **Rechecking Your Work is Important.**

  Always recheck your answers to math problems. Rechecking problems may be very helpful if you have time left at the end of the test.

- **You Can Draw a Table, Chart, or Picture to Help You Answer the Question.**

  Diagramming or drawing what you already know can help you find the right answer.

Consider this example:

1 Marcus and his three friends are looking for a snack. They find five different types of ice cream: chocolate chip, fudge ripple, strawberry, vanilla, and orange sherbet in the freezer and five different cookies: chocolate chip, sugar, peanut butter, raisin, and oatmeal in the cookie jar. For each flavor of ice cream there is only enough for one serving, and only one cookie of each kind.

After his friends have made their choices, how many types of ice cream and cookies are left for Marcus to choose from?

A. 2 types of ice cream and 1 type of cookie

B. 2 types of ice cream and 2 types of cookies

C. 1 type of ice cream and 2 types of cookies

D. 1 type of ice cream and 1 type of cookie

By creating a diagram, you can see there are 2 types of ice cream and 2 types of cookies left for Marcus to choose from. Choice B is correct.

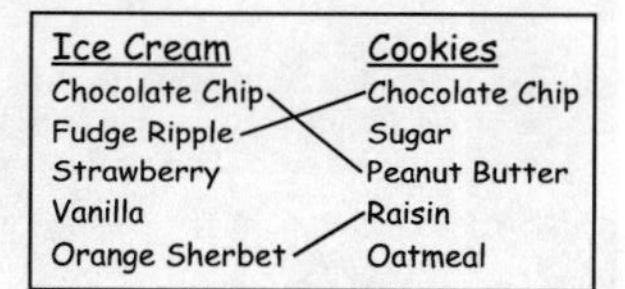

Specific Strategies for Online Tests

Kids usually have two different kinds of thoughts about taking a test on a computer. Some say, "Well, I use my computer all the time … I'm not going to even pay attention to the test … computers are easy!" Some kids think in the opposite way. They say, "A computer test? That has to be even scarier than a regular test … there is no way I am going to do well!" The truth is that both of them are wrong. You have to use some special strategies to do your best on computer tests, and when you do, you will do your best!

1. **Read the Directions.** Here is a silly question: Would you want to eat a cake your friend made if he didn't read the directions on the box? Probably not! But even if you aren't a famous cook, you could make a pretty good cake if you read and follow directions. If you read the directions for EACH QUESTION you will have a much better chance of showing what you know. Because even if you know a lot, you have to answer what the question asks. Don't leave out this important step to test success!

2. **Don't Go With the First Answer.** Take a little time and read the WHOLE question and ALL the answer choices. The first answer that looks right is not always the best. Think about going out to dinner with your grandmother. You look at the menu and see "Big Ole Burger"! That sounds good. But if you looked at ALL the menu choices, you might have found your favorite tacos! The burger was good, but if you took more time, you would have found a better choice.

3. **Ask Yourself … How Much Time Do I Have?** You will have a certain amount of time to complete each section of the test. Always check to see how much time you will have. Practice also helps. Did you know that football players practice and practice to see how long it takes to line up and start a play? After a while they are more relaxed and don't worry about time running out. You need to take some practice tests to feel comfortable with timed tests.

4. **Is There a Good Way to Guess?** Most of the time it is a good idea to guess, especially if you can make an "educated" guess! That means you know some things about the question, but not everything. Remember to use your common sense, as well as other information you know, to help you make an "educated guess."

5. **When Should You Guess?** Unless the directions say that you will lose points for guessing, go for it! Educated guesses are the best, but even if you are really unsure of the answer, calm down and take a guess. If you have four possible answers, and make a guess, you have a one out of four chance of guessing correctly. That is like having three old pennies and one new penny in a bowl. If you just reach in, you will get the new penny one out of every four times you try. That's why you should answer every question!

6. **Don't Mess With That Test Window!** When people get a little nervous, they tend to make silly mistakes. One kid was rushing to make some toast before running off to school, and he unplugged the toaster instead of making the toast! Figure out how the computer screen works, and DON'T close that test window!

7. **Have a Good Attitude!** The better you feel, the better you will do! Remind yourself of how much you have learned in school. Remember that while this test is important, that your teachers will still like you a lot no matter how you do. Just do your best and feel good about yourself. Did you know that when runners have a good attitude, that they win more often? Well, the same goes for you and tests!

8. **If You Have Time Left, Use it!** You can use extra time to help you do your best! If your computer test allows, review your answers, especially if you guessed at a question or two. Take a deep breath and calm down. You might find that a better answer comes into your mind. Talk to yourself a little about some of your answers. You might ask yourself, "I chose the answer that said that it will take 6 hours for that ice cube to melt. That seems like a long time … maybe I better recheck this and see if that makes sense."

Sixth graders all over have good ideas about tests. Here are some of them!

- Ask yourself, "Did I answer the question that was asked?" Carefully read the question so you can give the right answer.
- Read each answer choice before filling in an answer bubble. Sometimes, you read the first choice, and it seems right. But, when you get to the third choice, you realize that's the correct answer. If you had stopped with the first choice, you would have answered the question incorrectly. It is important to read all four choices before answering the question.
- Remember, nobody is trying to trick you. Do not look for trick answers. There will always be a right answer. If the answer choices do not look right, mark the question and go back to it later.
- Don't look around the room. Don't worry about how fast your friends are working, and don't worry about how well they are doing. Only worry about yourself. If you do that, you will do better on the test.

Mathematics

Introduction

The Mathematics assessment reflects what students should know and should be able to do in the sixth grade. State Assessments assess students' knowledge with multiple-choice and constructed-response items. The questions are not meant to confuse or trick them but are written so students have the best opportunity to show what they know about mathematics.

The Mathematics chapter in the *Show What You Know® on the Common Core for Grade 6 Mathematics, Parent/Teacher Edition* contains the following:

- The Common Core State Standards for Grade 6.
- Two full-length Mathematics Assessments from the Student Workbook, in reduced-page format, with sample responses, correlation charts, a standards checklist, and a grading document.

Ratios and Proportional Relationships 6.RP

Understand ratio concepts and use ratio reasoning to solve problems.

1. Understand the concept of a ratio and use ratio language to describe a ratio relationship between two quantities. *For example, "The ratio of wings to beaks in the bird house at the zoo was 2:1, because for every 2 wings there was 1 beak." "For every vote candidate A received, candidate C received nearly three votes."*

2. Understand the concept of a unit rate *a/b* associated with a ratio *a:b* with $b \neq 0$, and use rate language in the context of a ratio relationship. *For example, "This recipe has a ratio of 3 cups of flour to 4 cups of sugar, so there is 3/4 cup of flour for each cup of sugar." "We paid $75 for 15 hamburgers, which is a rate of $5 per hamburger."(Expectations for unit rates in this grade are limited to non-complex fractions.)*

3. Use ratio and rate reasoning to solve real-world and mathematical problems, e.g., by reasoning about tables of equivalent ratios, tape diagrams, double number line diagrams, or equations.

    a. Make tables of equivalent ratios relating quantities with whole-number measurements, find missing values in the tables, and plot the pairs of values on the coordinate plane. Use tables to compare ratios.

    b. Solve unit rate problems including those involving unit pricing and constant speed. *For example, if it took 7 hours to mow 4 lawns, then at that rate, how many lawns could be mowed in 35 hours? At what rate were lawns being mowed?*

    c. Find a percent of a quantity as a rate per 100 (e.g., 30% of a quantity means 30/100 times the quantity); solve problems involving finding the whole, given a part and the percent.

    d. Use ratio reasoning to convert measurement units; manipulate and transform units appropriately when multiplying or dividing quantities.

The Number System 6.NS

Apply and extend previous understandings of multiplication and division to divide fractions by fractions.

1. Interpret and compute quotients of fractions, and solve word problems involving division of fractions by fractions, e.g., by using visual fraction models and equations to represent the problem. *For example, create a story context for (2/3) ÷ (3/4) and use a visual fraction model to show the quotient; use the relationship between multiplication and division to explain that (2/3) ÷ (3/4) = 8/9 because 3/4 of 8/9 is 2/3. (In general, (a/b) ÷ (c/d) = ad/bc.) How much chocolate will each person get if 3 people share 1/2 lb of chocolate equally? How many 3/4-cup servings are in 2/3 of a cup of yogurt? How wide is a rectangular strip of land with length 3/4 mi and area 1/2 square mi?*

Compute fluently with multi-digit numbers and find common factors and multiples.

2. Fluently divide multi-digit numbers using the standard algorithm.

3. Fluently add, subtract, multiply, and divide multi-digit decimals using the standard algorithm for each operation.

4. Find the greatest common factor of two whole numbers less than or equal to 100 and the least common multiple of two whole numbers less than or equal to 12. Use the distributive property to express a sum of two whole numbers 1–100 with a common factor as a multiple of a sum of two whole numbers with no common factor. *For example, express 36 + 8 as 4 (9 + 2).*

Apply and extend previous understandings of numbers to the system of rational numbers.

5. Understand that positive and negative numbers are used together to describe quantities having opposite directions or values (e.g., temperature above/below zero, elevation above/below sea level, credits/debits, positive/negative electric charge); use positive and negative numbers to represent quantities in real-world contexts, explaining the meaning of 0 in each situation.

6. Understand a rational number as a point on the number line. Extend number line diagrams and coordinate axes familiar from previous grades to represent points on the line and in the plane with negative number coordinates.

   a. Recognize opposite signs of numbers as indicating locations on opposite sides of 0 on the number line; recognize that the opposite of the opposite of a number is the number itself, e.g., -(-3) = 3, and that 0 is its own opposite.

   b. Understand signs of numbers in ordered pairs as indicating locations in quadrants of the coordinate plane; recognize that when two ordered pairs differ only by signs, the locations of the points are related by reflections across one or both axes.

   c. Find and position integers and other rational numbers on a horizontal or vertical number line diagram; find and position pairs of integers and other rational numbers on a coordinate plane.

7. Understand ordering and absolute value of rational numbers.

   a. Interpret statements of inequality as statements about the relative position of two numbers on a number line diagram. *For example, interpret -3 > -7 as a statement that -3 is located to the right of -7 on a number line oriented from left to right.*

   b. Write, interpret, and explain statements of order for rational numbers in real-world contexts. *For example, write -3°C > -7°C to express the fact that -3°C is warmer than -7°C.*

   c. Understand the absolute value of a rational number as its distance from 0 on the number line; interpret absolute value as magnitude for a positive or negative quantity in a real-world situation. *For example, for an account balance of -30 dollars, write |-30| = 30 to describe the size of the debt in dollars.*

   d. Distinguish comparisons of absolute value from statements about order. *For example, recognize that an account balance less than -30 dollars represents a debt greater than 30 dollars.*

8. Solve real-world and mathematical problems by graphing points in all four quadrants of the coordinate plane. Include use of coordinates and absolute value to find distances between points with the same first coordinate or the same second coordinate.

Expressions and Equations 6.EE

Apply and extend previous understandings of arithmetic to algebraic expressions.

1. Write and evaluate numerical expressions involving whole-number exponents.
2. Write, read, and evaluate expressions in which letters stand for numbers.
   a. Write expressions that record operations with numbers and with letters standing for numbers. *For example, express the calculation "Subtract y from 5" as* $5 - y$.
   b. Identify parts of an expression using mathematical terms (sum, term, product, factor, quotient, coefficient); view one or more parts of an expression as a single entity. *For example, describe the expression* $2\ (8 + 7)$ *as a product of two factors; view* $(8 + 7)$ *as both a single entity and a sum of two terms.*
   c. Evaluate expressions at specific values of their variables. Include expressions that arise from formulas used in real-world problems. Perform arithmetic operations, including those involving whole-number exponents, in the conventional order when there are no parentheses to specify a particular order (Order of Operations). *For example, use the formulas* $V = s^3$ *and* $A = 6\ s^2$ *to find the volume and surface area of a cube with sides of length* $s = 1/2$.
3. Apply the properties of operations to generate equivalent expressions. *For example, apply the distributive property to the expression* $3\ (2 + x)$ *to produce the equivalent expression* $6 + 3x$*; apply the distributive property to the expression* $24x + 18y$ *to produce the equivalent expression* $6\ (4x + 3y)$*; apply properties of operations to* $y + y + y$ *to produce the equivalent expression* $3y$.
4. Identify when two expressions are equivalent (i.e., when the two expressions name the same number regardless of which value is substituted into them). *For example, the expressions* $y + y + y$ *and* $3y$ *are equivalent because they name the same number regardless of which number y stands for.*

Reason about and solve one-variable equations and inequalities.

5. Understand solving an equation or inequality as a process of answering a question: which values from a specified set, if any, make the equation or inequality true? Use substitution to determine whether a given number in a specified set makes an equation or inequality true.
6. Use variables to represent numbers and write expressions when solving a real-world or mathematical problem; understand that a variable can represent an unknown number, or, depending on the purpose at hand, any number in a specified set.
7. Solve real-world and mathematical problems by writing and solving equations of the form $x + p = q$ and $px = q$ for cases in which p, q and x are all nonnegative rational numbers.
8. Write an inequality of the form $x > c$ or $x < c$ to represent a constraint or condition in a real-world or mathematical problem. Recognize that inequalities of the form $x > c$ or $x < c$ have infinitely many solutions; represent solutions of such inequalities on number line diagrams.

Represent and analyze quantitative relationships between dependent and independent variables.

9. Use variables to represent two quantities in a real-world problem that change in relationship to one another; write an equation to express one quantity, thought of as the dependent variable, in terms of the other quantity, thought of as the independent variable. Analyze the relationship between the dependent and independent variables using graphs and tables, and relate these to the equation. *For example, in a problem involving motion at constant speed, list and graph ordered pairs of distances and times, and write the equation $d = 65t$ to represent the relationship between distance and time.*

Geometry 6.G

Solve real-world and mathematical problems involving area, surface area, and volume.

1. Find the area of right triangles, other triangles, special quadrilaterals, and polygons by composing into rectangles or decomposing into triangles and other shapes; apply these techniques in the context of solving real-world and mathematical problems.
2. Find the volume of a right rectangular prism with fractional edge lengths by packing it with unit cubes of the appropriate unit fraction edge lengths, and show that the volume is the same as would be found by multiplying the edge lengths of the prism. Apply the formulas $V = l\,wh$ and $V = bh$ to find volumes of right rectangular prisms with fractional edge lengths in the context of solving real-world and mathematical problems.
3. Draw polygons in the coordinate plane given coordinates for the vertices; use coordinates to find the length of a side joining points with the same first coordinate or the same second coordinate. Apply these techniques in the context of solving real-world and mathematical problems.
4. Represent three-dimensional figures using nets made up of rectangles and triangles, and use the nets to find the surface area of these figures. Apply these techniques in the context of solving real-world and mathematical problems.

Statistics and Probability 6.SP

Develop understanding of statistical variability.

1. Recognize a statistical question as one that anticipates variability in the data related to the question and accounts for it in the answers. *For example, "How old am I?" is not a statistical question, but "How old are the students in my school?" is a statistical question because one anticipates variability in students' ages.*
2. Understand that a set of data collected to answer a statistical question has a distribution which can be described by its center, spread, and overall shape.
3. Recognize that a measure of center for a numerical data set summarizes all of its values with a single number, while a measure of variation describes how its values vary with a single number.

Summarize and describe distributions.

4. Display numerical data in plots on a number line, including dot plots, histograms, and box plots.
5. Summarize numerical data sets in relation to their context, such as by:
   a. Reporting the number of observations.
   b. Describing the nature of the attribute under investigation, including how it was measured and its units of measurement.
   c. Giving quantitative measures of center (median and/or mean) and variability (interquartile range and/or mean absolute deviation), as well as describing any overall pattern and any striking deviations from the overall pattern with reference to the context in which the data were gathered.
   d. Relating the choice of measures of center and variability to the shape of the data distribution and the context in which the data were gathered.

Glossary

addend: Numbers added together to give a sum. For example, 2 + 7 = 9. The numbers 2 and 7 are addends.

addition: An operation joining two or more sets where the result is the whole.

a.m.: The hours from midnight to noon; from Latin words *ante meridiem* meaning "before noon."

analyze: To break down information into parts so that it may be more easily understood.

angle: A figure formed by two rays that meet at the same end point called a vertex. Angles can be obtuse, acute, right, or straight.

area: The number of square units needed to cover a region. The most common abbreviation for area is *A*.

Associative Property of Addition: The grouping of addends can be changed and the sum will be the same.
Example: (3 + 1) + 2 = 6; 3 + (1 + 2) = 6.

Associative Property of Multiplication: The grouping of factors can be changed and the product will be the same.
Example: (3 x 2) x 4 = 24; 3 x (2 x 4) = 24.

attribute: A characteristic or distinctive feature.

average: A number found by adding two or more quantities together and then dividing the sum by the number of quantities. For example, in the set {9, 5, 4}, the average is 6: 9 + 5 + 4 = 18; 18 ÷ 3 = 6. *See mean.*

axes: Plural of axis. Perpendicular lines used as reference lines in a coordinate system or graph; traditionally, the horizontal axis (*x*-axis) represents the independent variable and the vertical axis (*y*-axis) represents the dependent variable.

bar graph: A graph using bars to show data.

capacity: The amount an object holds when filled.

chart: A way to show information, such as in a graph or table.

circle: A closed, curved line made up of points that are all the same distance from a point inside called the center.
Example: A circle with center point *P* is shown below.

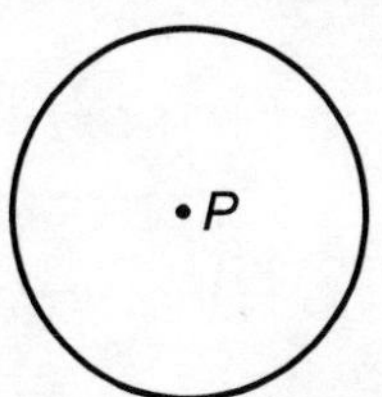

circle graph: Sometimes called a pie chart; a way of representing data that shows the fractional part or percentage of an overall set as an appropriately-sized wedge of a circle.
Example:

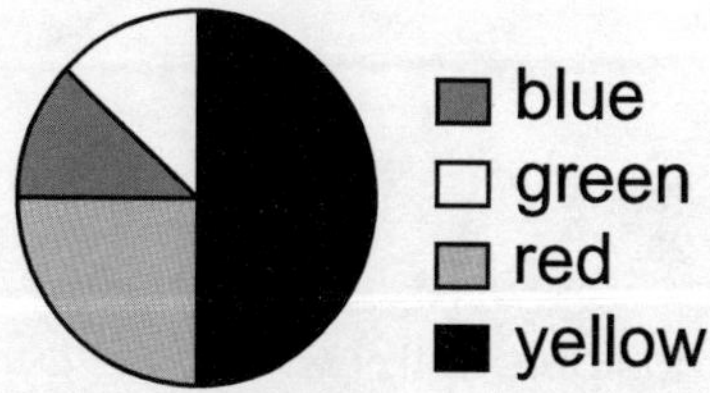

circumference: The boundary line or perimeter of a circle; also, the length of the perimeter of a circle.
Example:

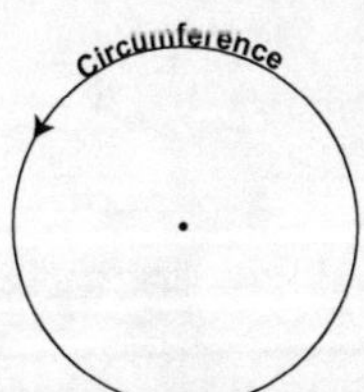

Commutative Property of Addition: Numbers can be added in any order and the sum will be the same.
Example: 3 + 4 = 4 + 3.

Commutative Property of Multiplication: Numbers can be multiplied in any order and the product will be the same.
Example: 3 x 6 = 6 x 3.

compare: To look for similarities and differences. For example, is one number greater than, less than, or equal to another number?

conclusion: A statement that follows logically from other facts.

Glossary

cone: A solid figure with a circle as its base and a curved surface that meets at a point.

cones

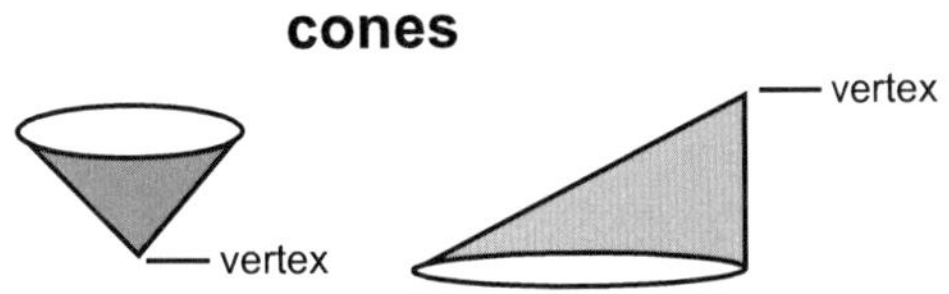

congruent figures: Figures that have the same shape and size.

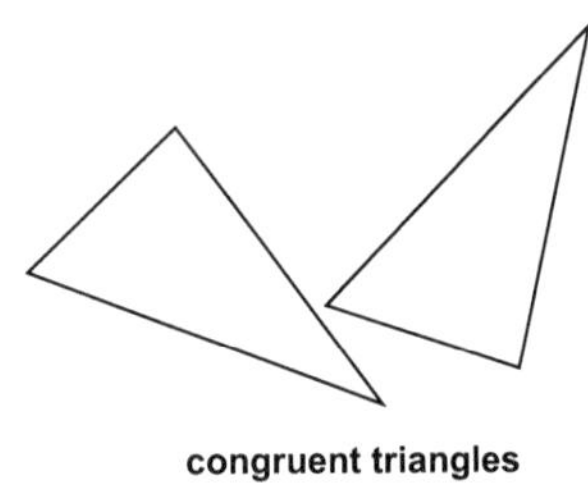

congruent triangles

cube: A solid figure with six faces that are congruent (equal) squares.

cylinder: A solid figure with two circular bases that are congruent (equal) and parallel to each other connected by a curved lateral surface.

data: Information that is collected.

decimal number: A number expressed in base 10, such as 39,456, where each digit's value is determined by multiplying it by some power of 10.

denominator: The bottom number in a fraction.

diagram: A drawing that represents a mathematical situation.

difference: The answer when subtracting two numbers.

distance: The amount of space between two points.

dividend: A number in a division problem that is divided. Dividend ÷ divisor = quotient. Example: In 15 ÷ 3 = 5, 15 is the dividend.

quotient / divisor)dividend   5 / 3)15

divisible: A number that can be divided by another number without leaving a remainder. Example: 12 is divisible by 3 because 12 ÷ 3 is an integer, namely 4.

division: An operation that tells how many equal groups there are or how many are in each group.

divisor: The number by which another number is divided. Example: In 15 ÷ 3 = 5, 3 is the divisor.

quotient / divisor)dividend   5 / 3)15

edge: The line segment where two faces of a solid figure meet.

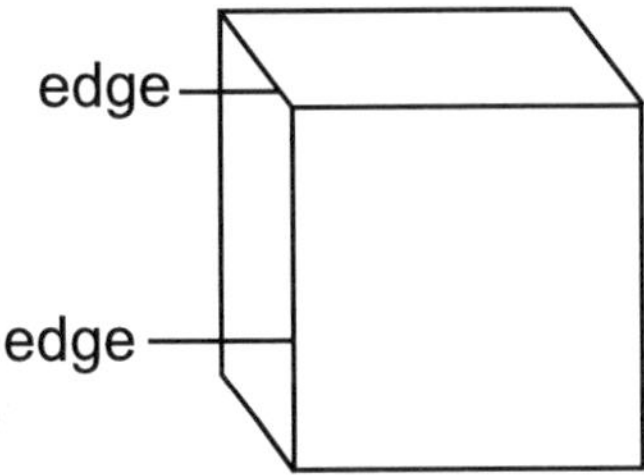

equivalent fractions: Two fractions with equal values.

equality: Two or more sets of values that are equal.

equation: A number sentence that says two expressions are equal (=). Example: 4 + 8 = 6 + 6.

estimate: To find an approximate value or measurement of something without exact calculation.

even number: A whole number that has a 0, 2, 4, 6, or 8 in the ones place. A number that is a multiple of 2. Examples: 0, 4, and 678 are even numbers.

expanded form: A number written as the sum of the values of its digits. Example: 546 = 500 + 40 + 6.

expression: A combination of variables, numbers, and symbols that represent a mathematical relationship.

Glossary

face: The sides of a solid figure. For example, a cube has six faces that are all squares. The pyramid below has five faces—four triangles and one square.

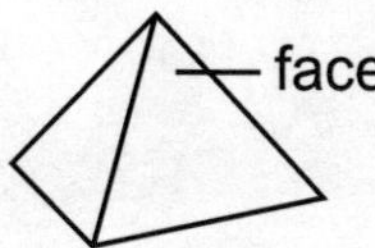

fact family: A group of related facts using the same numbers.
Example: 5 + 8 = 13; 13 – 8 = 5.

factor: One of two or more numbers that are multiplied together to give a product.
Example: In 4 x 3 = 12, 4 and 3 are factors of 12.

figure: A geometric figure is a set of points and/or lines in 2 or 3 dimensions.

flip (reflection): The change in a position of a figure that is the result of picking it up and turning it over. Example: Reversing a "b" to a "d." Tipping a "p" to a "b" or a "b" to a "p" as shown below:

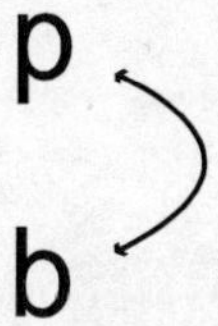

fraction: A symbol, such as $\frac{2}{8}$ or $\frac{5}{3}$, used to name a part of a whole, a part of a set, or a location on the number line.
Examples:

$$\frac{\text{numerator}}{\text{denominator}} = \frac{\text{dividend}}{\text{divisor}}$$

$$\frac{\text{\# of parts under consideration}}{\text{\# of parts in a set}}$$

function machine: Applies a function rule to a set of numbers, which determines a corresponding set of numbers.
Example: Input 9 → Rule x 7 → Output 63. If you apply the function rule "multiply by 7" to the values 5, 7, and 9, the corresponding values are:

5 → 35
7 → 49
9 → 63

graph: A "picture" showing how certain facts are related to each other or how they compare to one another. Some examples of types of graphs are line graphs, pie charts, bar graphs, scatterplots, and pictographs.

grid: A pattern of regularly spaced horizontal and vertical lines on a plane that can be used to locate points and graph equations.

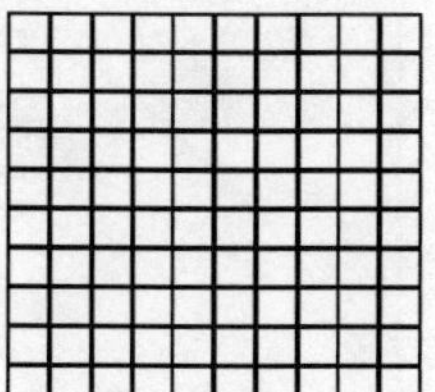

hexagon: A six-sided polygon. The total measure of the angles within a hexagon is 720°.

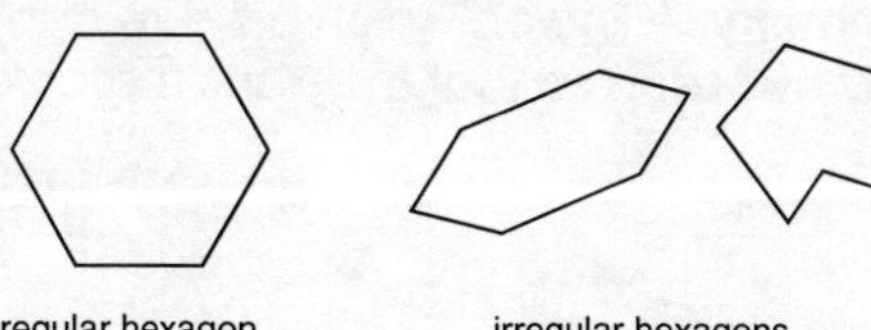

impossible event: An event that can never happen.

integer: Any number, positive or negative, that is a whole number distance away from zero on a number line, in addition to zero. Specifically, an integer is any number in the set {. . .-3,-2,-1, 0, 1, 2, 3. . .}.
Examples of integers include: 1, 5, 273, -2, -35, and -1,375.

intersecting lines: Lines that cross at a point.
Examples:

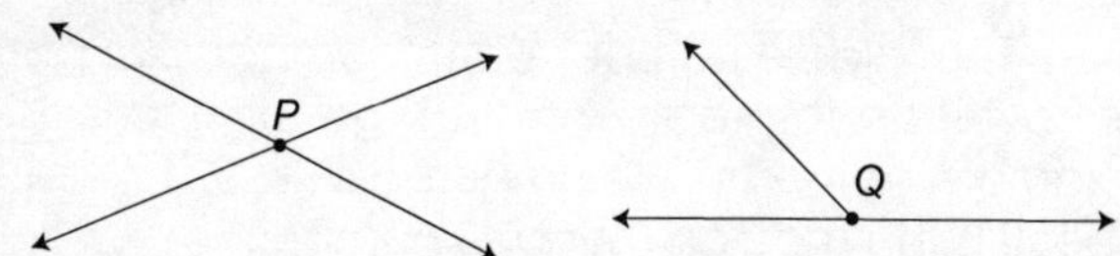

isosceles triangle: A triangle with at least two sides the same length.

justify: To prove or show to be true or valid using logic and/or evidence.

key: An explanation of what each symbol represents in a pictograph.

Glossary

kilometer (km): A metric unit of length: 1 kilometer = 1,000 meters.

line: A straight path of points that goes on forever in both directions.

line graph: A graph that uses a line or a curve to show how data changes over time.

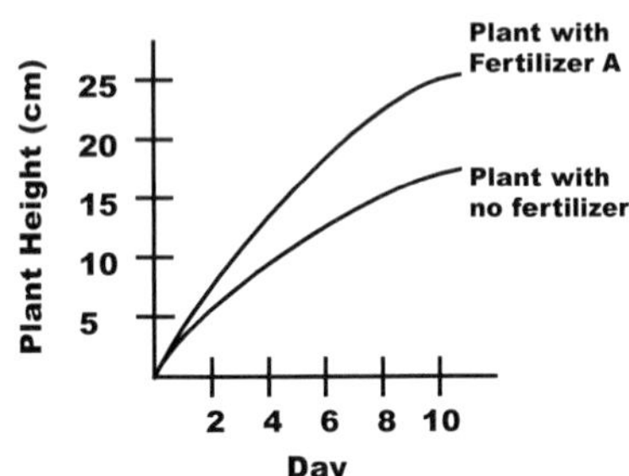

line of symmetry: A line on which a figure can be folded into two parts so that the parts match exactly.

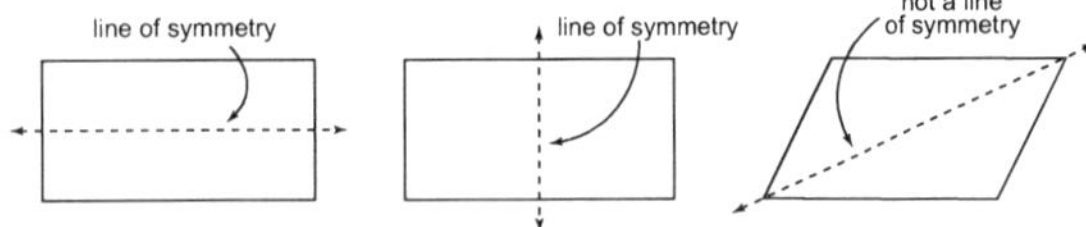

liter (L): A metric unit of capacity: 1 liter = 1,000 milliliters.

mass: The amount of matter an object has.

mean: Also called arithmetic average. A number found by adding two or more quantities together, and then dividing the sum by the number of quantities. For example, in the set {9, 5, 4} the mean is 6: 9 + 5 + 4 = 18; 18 ÷ 3 = 6. *See average.*

median: The middle number when numbers are put in order from least to greatest or from greatest to least. For example, in the set of numbers 6, 7, 8, 9, 10, the number 8 is the median (middle) number.

meter (m): A metric unit of length: 1 meter = 100 centimeters.

method: A systematic way of accomplishing a task.

mixed number: A number consisting of a whole number and a fraction.
Example: $6\frac{2}{3}$.

mode: The number or numbers that occur most often in a set of data. Example: The mode of {1, 3, 4, 5, 5, 7, 9} is 5.

multiple: A product of a number and any other whole number. Examples: {2, 4, 6, 8, 10, 12,...} are multiples of 2.

multiplication: An operation on two numbers that tells how many in all. The first number is the number of sets and the second number tells how many in each set.

number line: A line that shows numbers in order using a scale. Equal intervals are marked and usually labeled on the number line.

number sentence: An expression of a relationship between quantities as an equation or an inequality. Examples: 7 + 7 = 8 + 6; 14 < 92; 56 + 4 > 59.

numerator: The top number in a fraction.

octagon: An eight-sided polygon. The total measure of the angles within an octagon is 1080°.

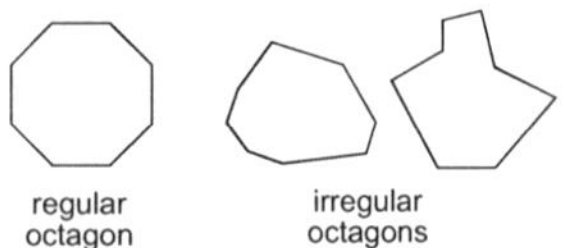

odd number: A whole number that has 1, 3, 5, 7, or 9 in the ones place. An odd number is not divisible by 2. Examples: The numbers 53 and 701 are odd numbers.

operation: A mathematical process that combines numbers; basic operations of arithmetic include addition, subtraction, multiplication, and division.

order: To arrange numbers from the least to greatest or from the greatest to least.

ordered pair: Two numbers inside a set of parentheses separated by a comma that are used to name a point on a coordinate grid.

parallel lines: Lines in the same plane that never intersect.

parallelogram: A quadrilateral in which opposite sides are parallel.

pattern: An arrangement of numbers, pictures, etc., in an organized and predictable way. Examples: 3, 6, 9, 12, or ® 0 ® 0 ® 0.

Glossary

pentagon: A five-sided polygon. The total measure of the angles within a pentagon is 540°.

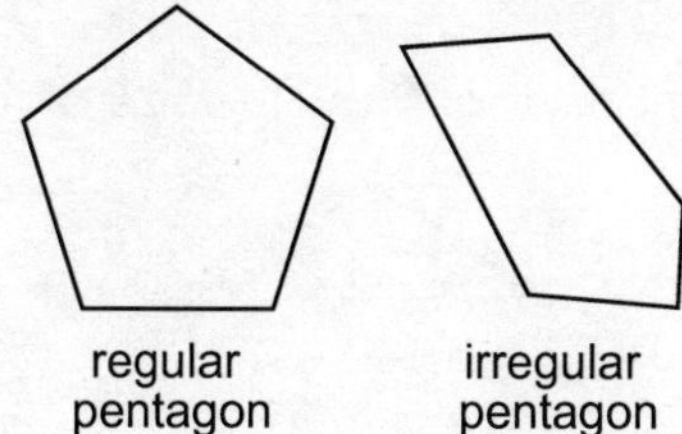

perimeter: The distance around a figure.

perpendicular lines: Two lines that intersect to form a right angle (90 degrees).

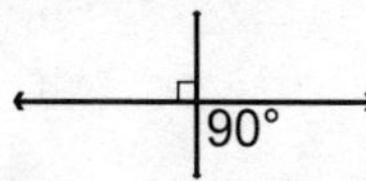

pictograph: A graph that uses pictures or symbols to represent similar data. The value of each picture is interpreted by a "key" or "legend."

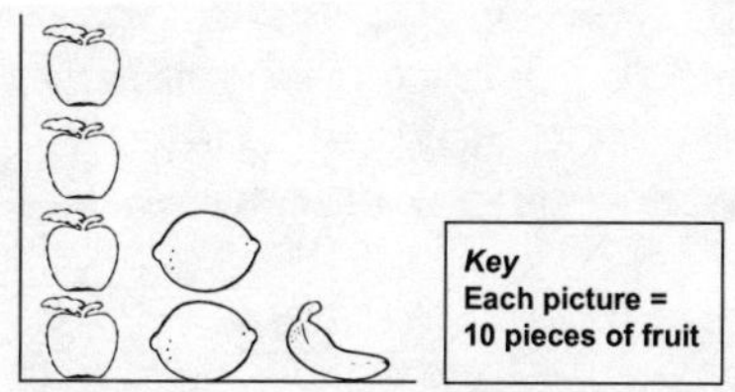

place value: The value given to the place a digit has in a number.
Example: In the number 135, the 1 is in the hundreds place so it represents 100 (1 x 100); the 3 is in the tens place so it represents 30 (3 x 10); and the 5 is in the ones place so it represents 5 (5 x 1).

p.m.: The hours from noon to midnight; from the Latin words *post meridiem* meaning "after noon."

point: An exact position often marked by a dot.

polygon: A closed figure made up of straight line segments.

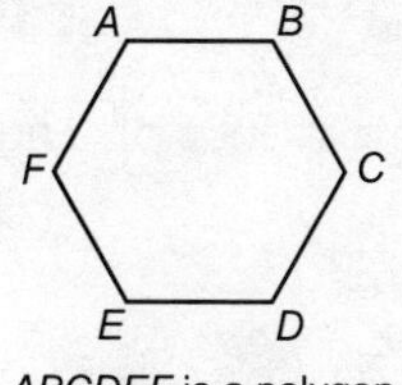

ABCDEF is a polygon.

possible event: An event that might or might not happen.

predict: To tell what you believe may happen in the future.

prediction: A prediction is a description of what may happen before it happens.

probability: The likelihood that something will happen.

product: The answer to a multiplication problem.
Example: In 3 x 4 = 12, 12 is the product.

pyramid: A solid figure in which the base is a polygon and faces are triangles with a common point called a vertex.

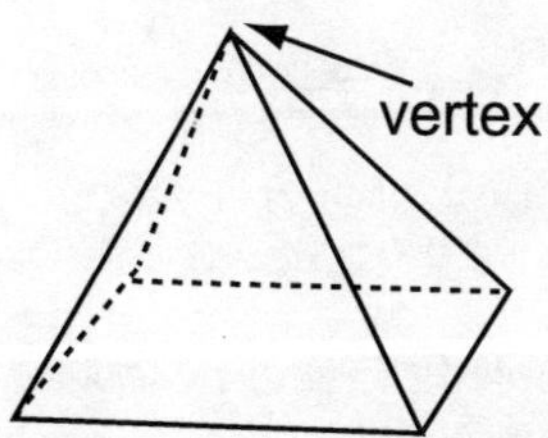

quadrilateral: A four-sided polygon. Rectangles, squares, parallelograms, rhombi, and trapezoids are all quadrilaterals. The total measure of the angles within a quadrilateral is 360°.
Example: *ABCD* is a quadrilateral.

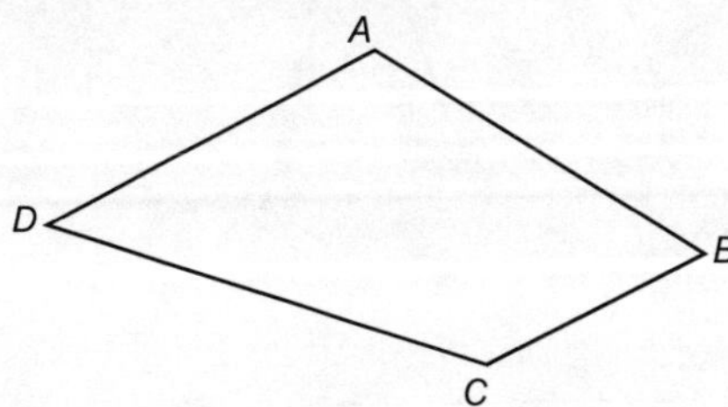

questionnaire: A set of questions for a survey.

quotient: The answer in a division problem.
Dividend ÷ divisor = quotient.
Example: In 15 ÷ 3 = 5, 5 is the quotient.

range: The difference between the least number and the greatest number in a data set. For example, in the set {4, 7, 10, 12, 36, 7, 2}, the range is 34; the greatest number (36) minus the least number (2): (36 – 2 = 34).

Glossary

rectangle: A quadrilateral with four right angles. A square is one example of a rectangle.

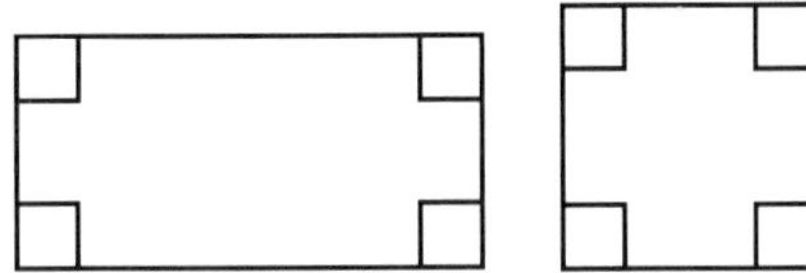

reflection: The change in the position of a figure that is the result of picking it up and turning it over. *See flip.*

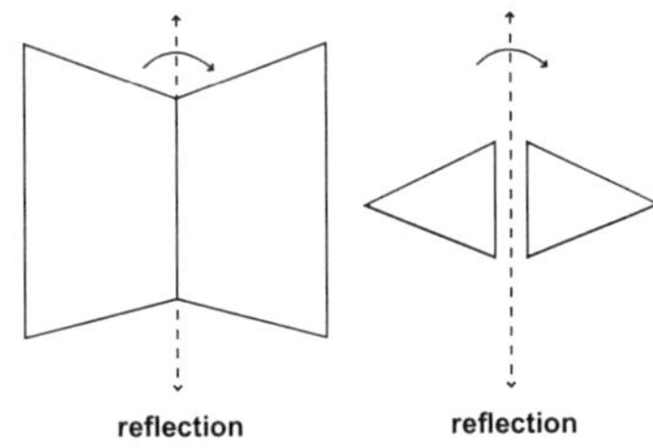

remainder: The number that is left over after dividing. Example: In 31 ÷ 7 = 4 R 3, the 3 is the remainder.

represent: To present clearly; describe; show.

rhombus: A quadrilateral with opposite sides parallel and all sides the same length. A square is one kind of rhombus.

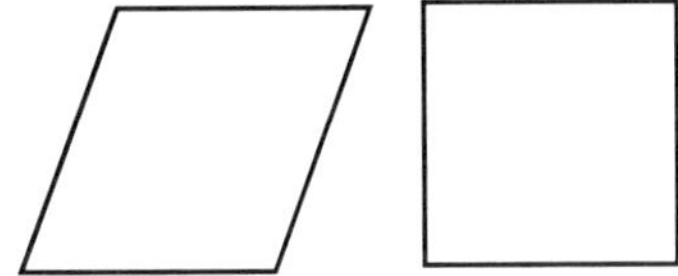

right angle: An angle that forms a square corner and measures 90 degrees.

right triangle: A triangle having one right angle. *See right angle and triangle.*

rounding: Replacing an exact number with a number that tells about how much or how many to the nearest ten, hundred, thousand, and so on.
Example: 52 rounded to the nearest 10 is 50.

rule: A procedure; a prescribed method; a way of describing the relationship between two sets of numbers. Example: In the following data, the rule is to add 3:

Input	Output
3	6
5	8
9	12

ruler: A straight-edged instrument used for measuring the lengths of objects. A ruler usually measures smaller units of length, such as inches or centimeters.

scale: The numbers that show the size of the units used on a graph.

sequence: A set of numbers arranged in a special order or pattern.

set: A group made up of numbers, figures, or parts.

side: A line segment connected to other segments to form the boundary of a polygon.

similar: A description for figures that have the same shape.

slide (translation): The change in the position of a figure that moves up, down, or sideways.
Example: scooting a book on a table.

solids: Figures in three dimensions.

solve: To find the solution to an equation or problem; finding the values of unknown variables that will make a true mathematical statement.

sphere: A solid figure in the shape of a ball.
Example: a basketball is a sphere.

square: A rectangle with congruent (equal) sides. *See rectangle.*

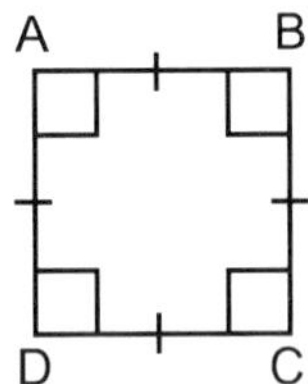

square number: The product of a number multiplied by itself.
Example: 49 is a square number (7 x 7 = 49).

square unit: A square with sides 1 unit long, used to measure area.

Glossary

standard form: A way to write a number showing only its digits. Example: 2,389.

standard units of measure: Units of measure commonly used; generally classified in the U.S. as the customary system or the metric system:

Customary System:

Length
1 foot (ft) = 12 inches (in)
1 yard (yd) = 3 feet or 36 inches
1 mile (mi) = 1,760 yards or 5,280 feet

Weight
16 ounces (oz) = 1 pound (lb)
2,000 pounds = 1 ton (t)

Capacity
1 pint (pt) = 2 cups (c)
1 quart (qt) = 2 pints
1 gallon (gal) = 4 quarts

Metric System:

Length
1 centimeter (cm) = 10 millimeters (mm)
1 decimeter (dm) = 10 centimeters
1 meter (m) = 100 centimeters
1 kilometer (km) = 1,000 meters

Weight
1,000 milligrams (mg) = 1 gram (g)
1,000 grams (g) = 1 kilogram (kg)
1,000 kilograms (kg) = 1 tonne (metric ton)

Capacity
1 liter (l) = 1,000 milliliters (ml)

strategy: A plan used in problem solving, such as looking for a pattern, drawing a diagram, working backward, etc.

subtraction: The operation that finds the difference between two numbers.

sum: The answer when adding two or more addends. Addend + Addend = Sum.

summary: A series of statements containing evidence, facts, and/or procedures that support a result.

survey: A way to collect data by asking a certain number of people the same question and recording their answers.

symmetry: A figure has line symmetry if it can be folded along a line so that both parts match exactly. A figure has radial or rotational symmetry if, after a rotation of less than 360°, it is indistinguishable from its former image.

Examples of Figures With At Least Two Lines of Symmetry

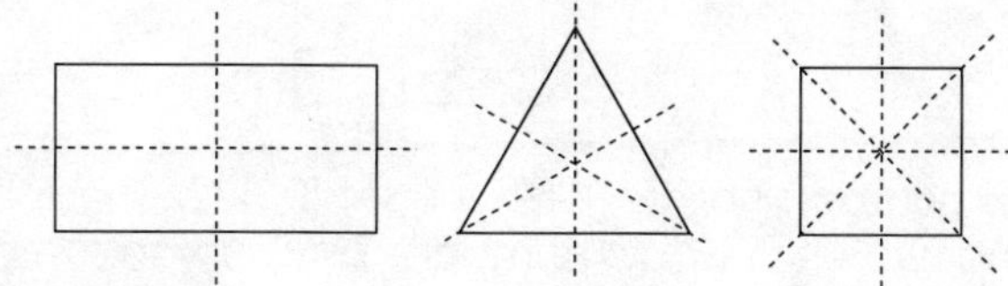

table: A method of displaying data in rows and columns.

temperature: A measure of hot or cold in degrees.

translation (slide): A change in the position of a figure that moves it up, down, or sideways.

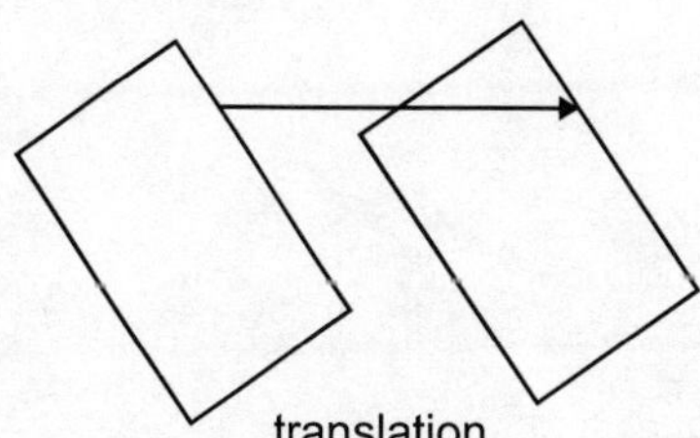

translation

triangle: A polygon with three sides. The sum of the angles of a triangle is always equal to 180°.

turn: The change in the position of a figure that moves it around a point. Also called a rotation.
Example: The hands of a clock turn around the center of the clock in a clockwise direction.

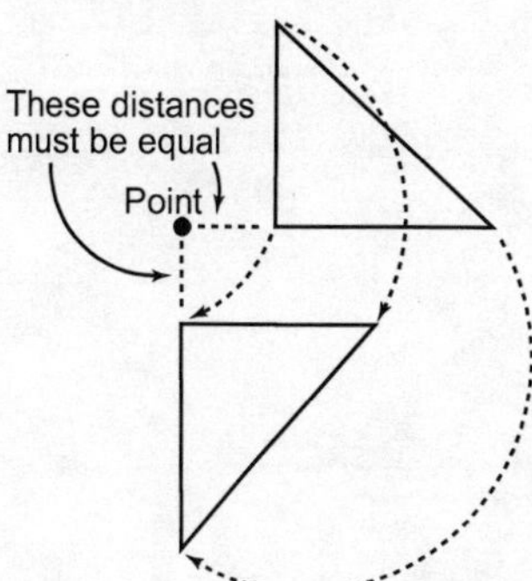

Glossary

unlikely event: An event that probably will not happen.

vertex: The point where two rays meet to form an angle or where the sides of a polygon meet, or the point where 3 or more edges meet in a solid figure.

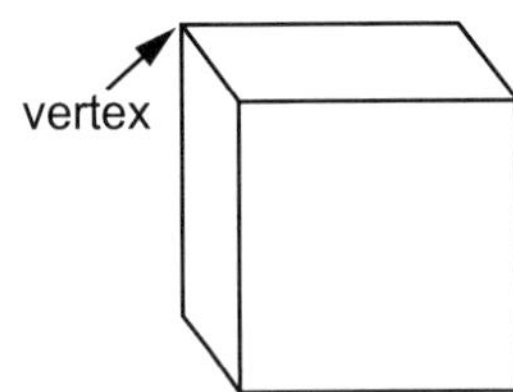

whole number: An integer in the set {0, 1, 2, 3 . . .}. In other words, a whole number is any number used when counting in addition to zero.

word forms: The number written in words. Examples: 546 is "five hundred forty-six."

Examples of Common Two-Dimensional Geometric Shapes

Right Triangle

Isosceles Triangle

Equilateral Triangle

Square

Rectangle

Parallelogram

Rhombus

Trapezoid

Pentagon

Hexagon

Octagon

Circle

Examples of How Lines Interact

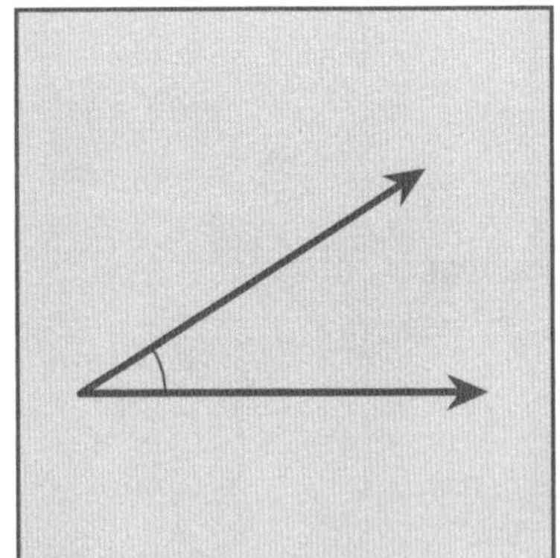

Acute Angle

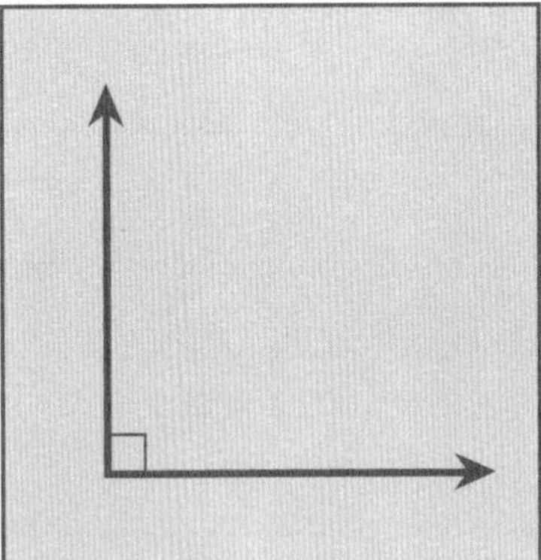

Right Angle

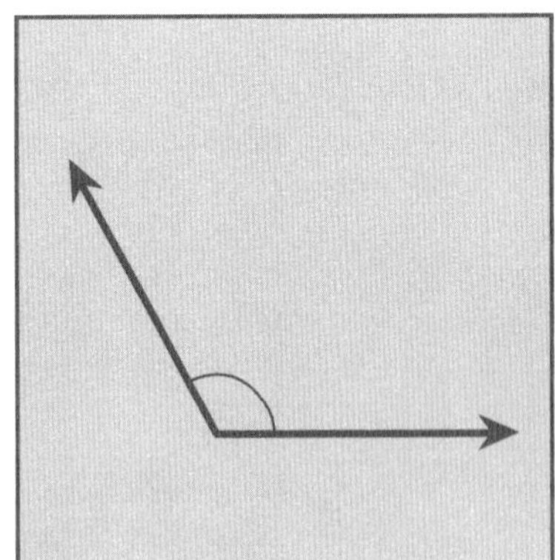

Obtuse Angle

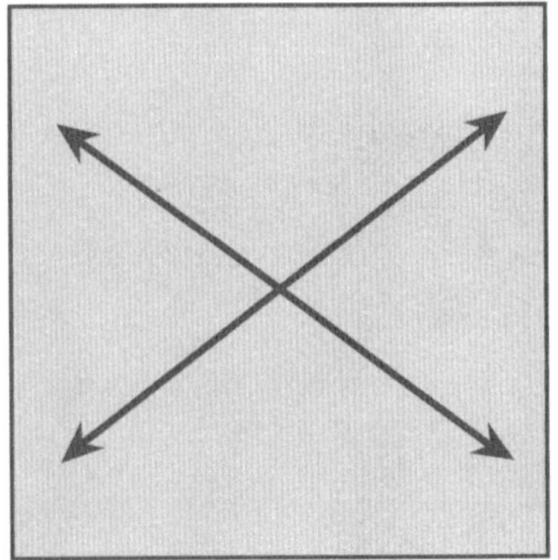

Intersecting

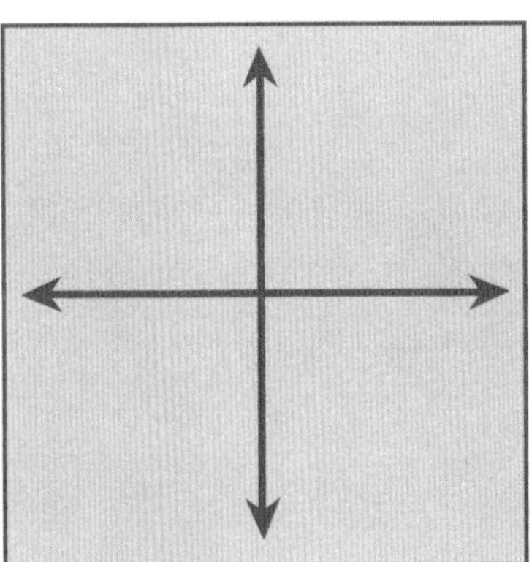

Perpendicular

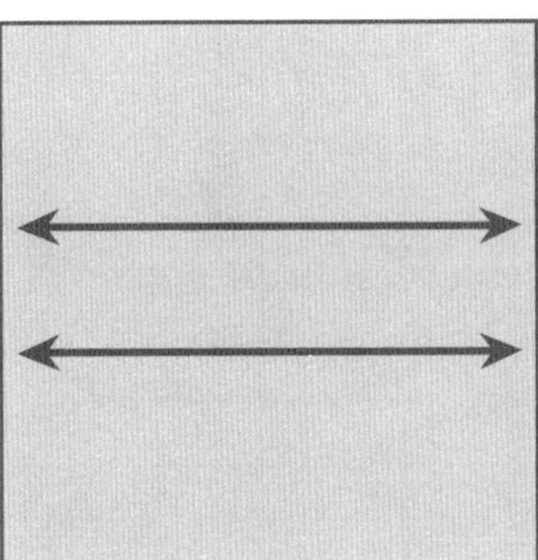

Parallel

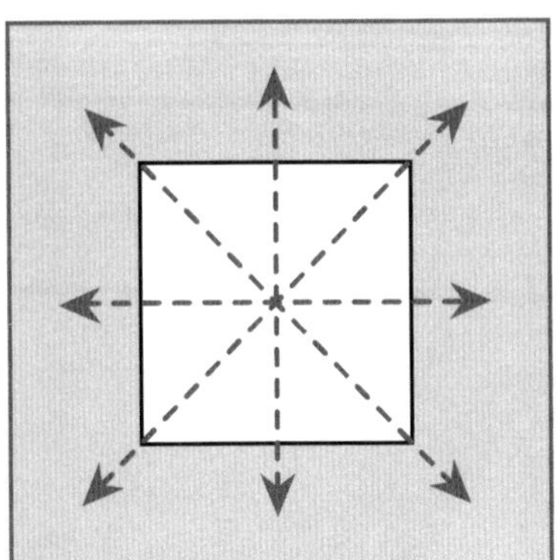

Lines of Symmetry

Examples of Common Types of Graphs

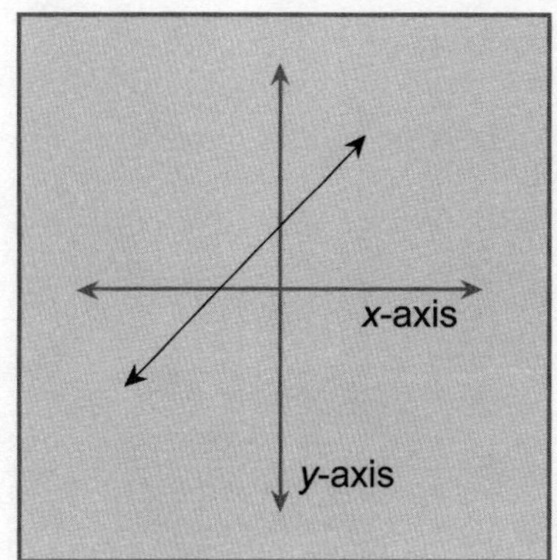

Line Graph

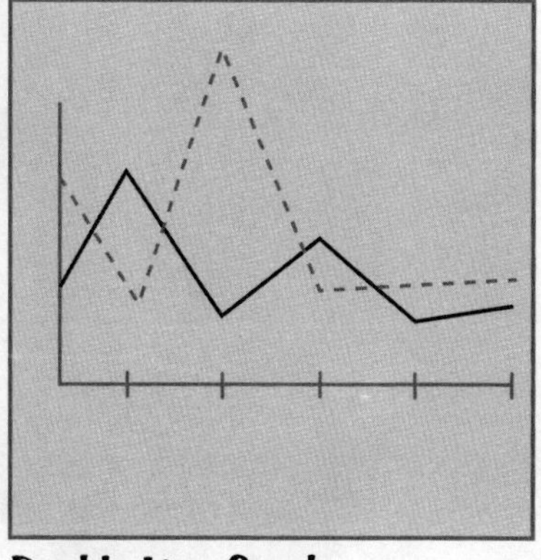

Double Line Graph

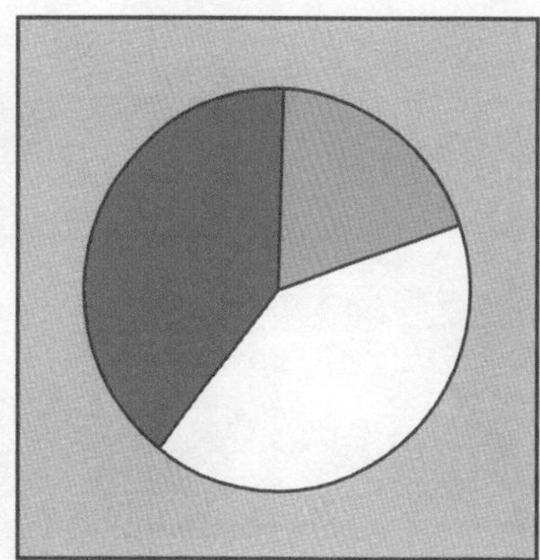

Pie Chart

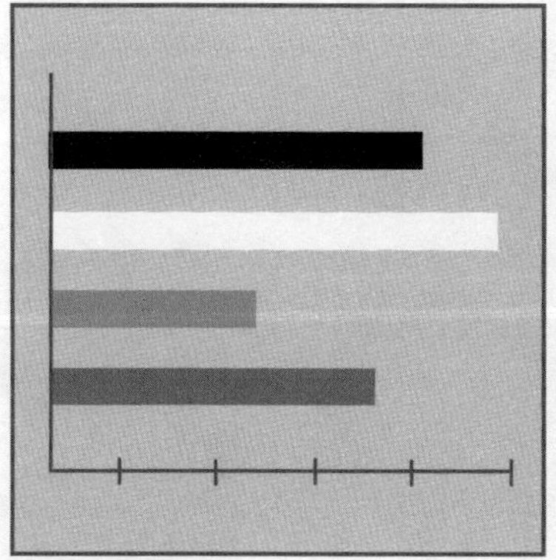

Bar Graph

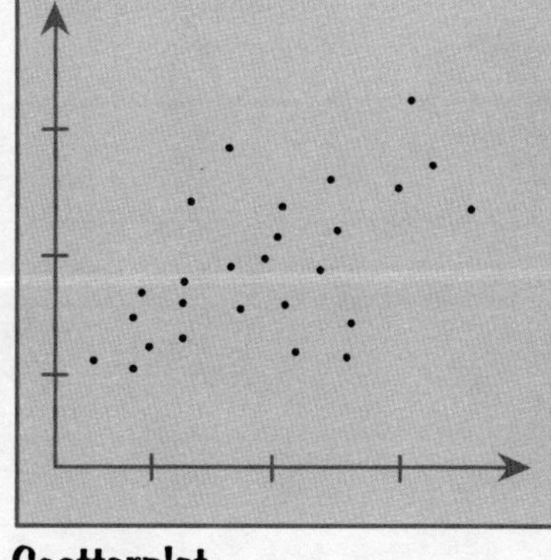

Scatterplot

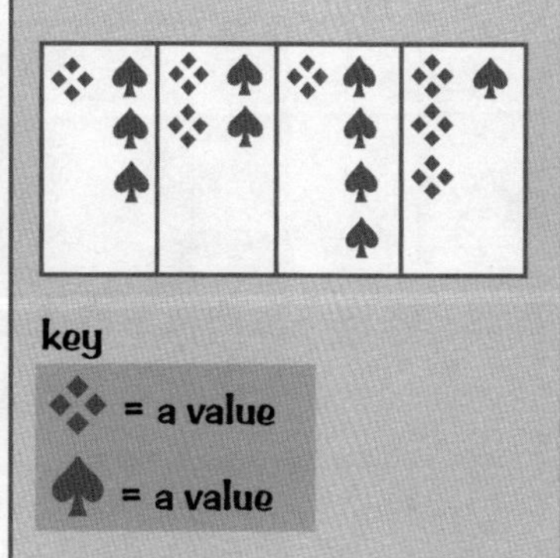

Pictograph

Examples of Common Three-Dimensional Objects

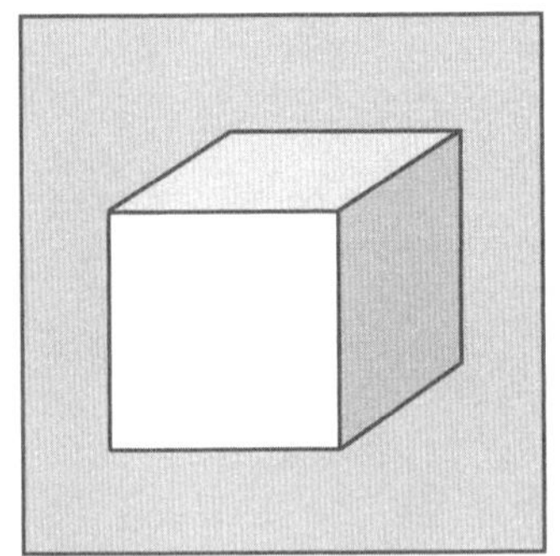
Cube

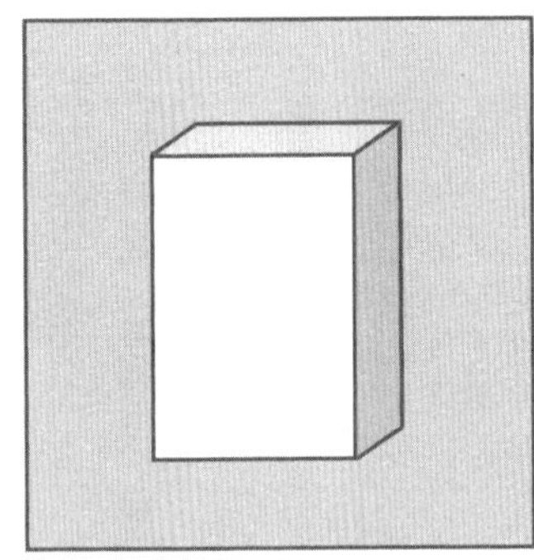
Rectangular Prism

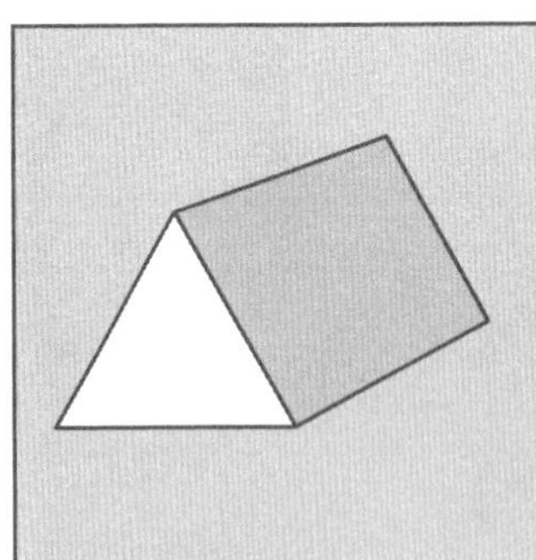
Triangular Prism

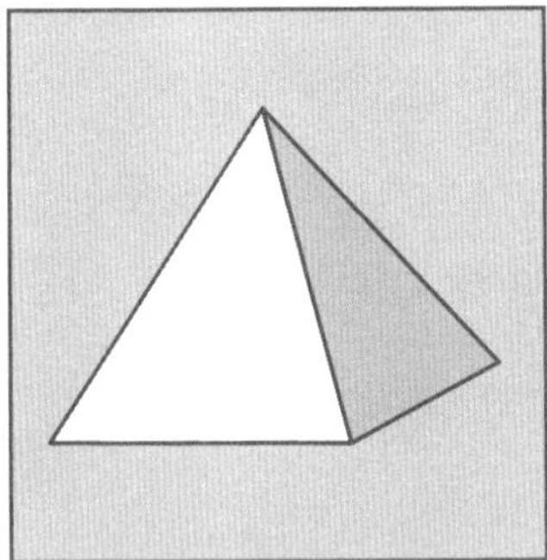
Pyramid

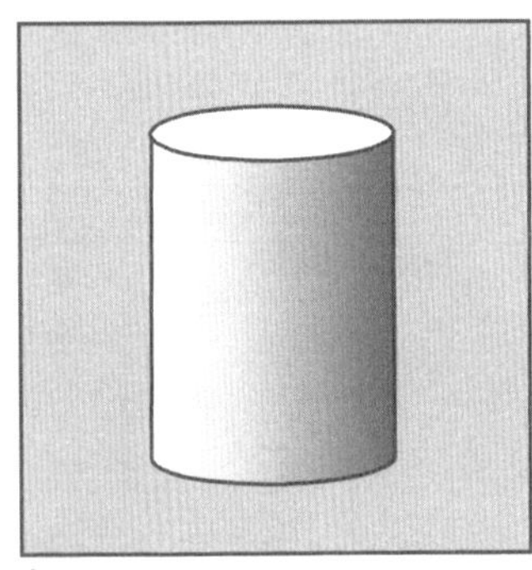
Cylinder

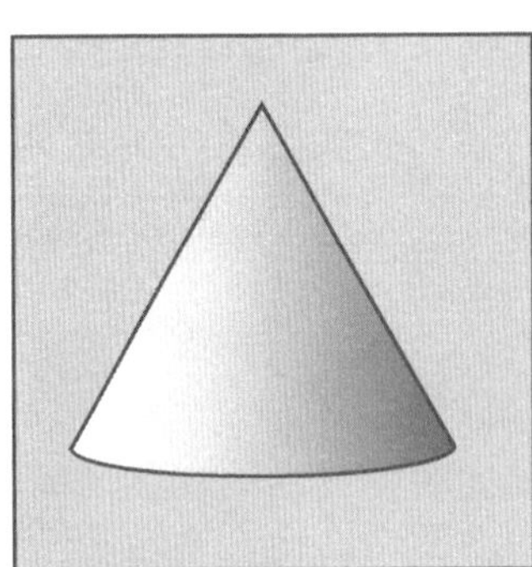
Cone

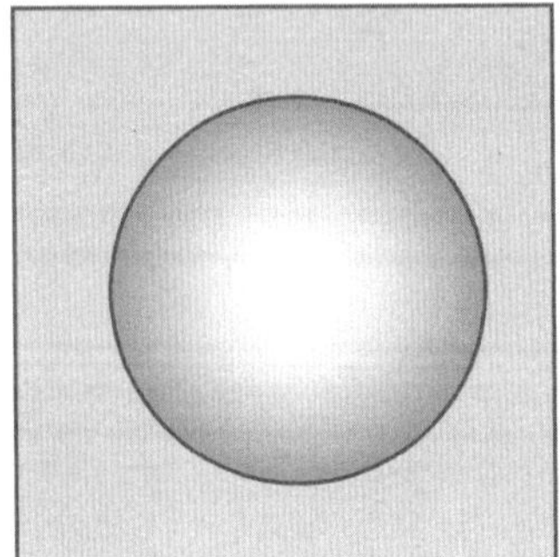
Sphere

Examples of Object Movement

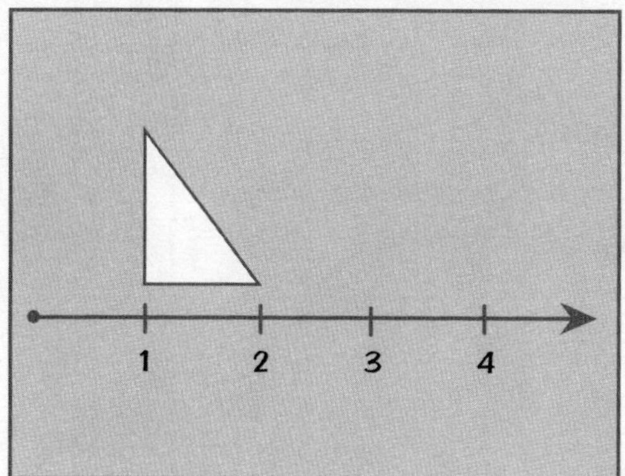

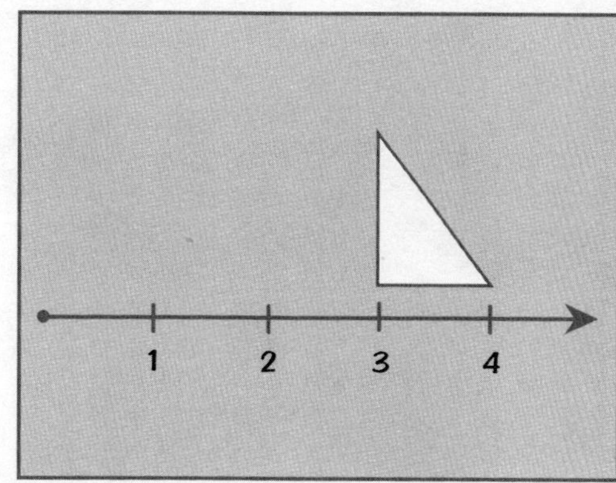

Translation

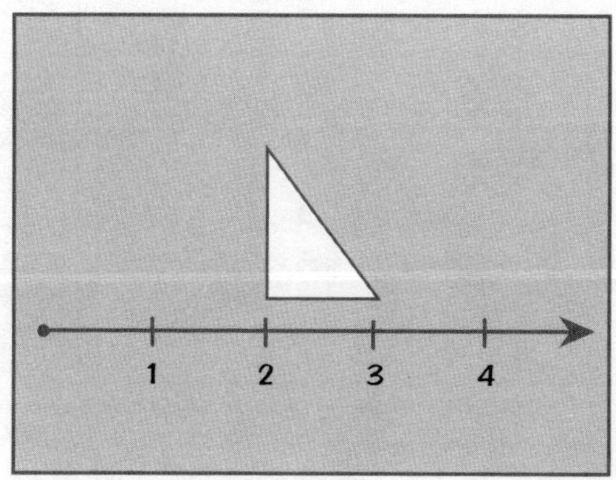

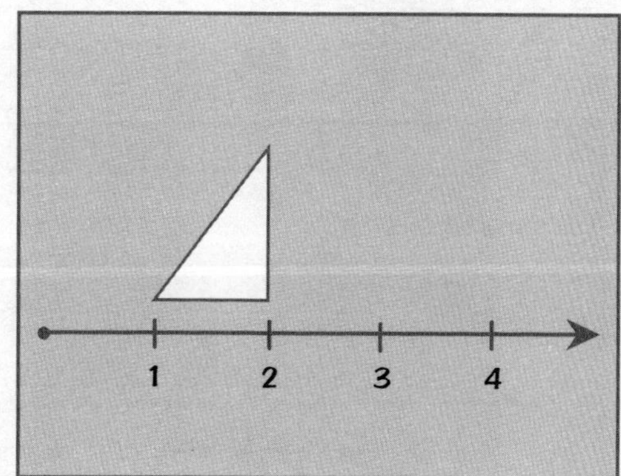

Reflection

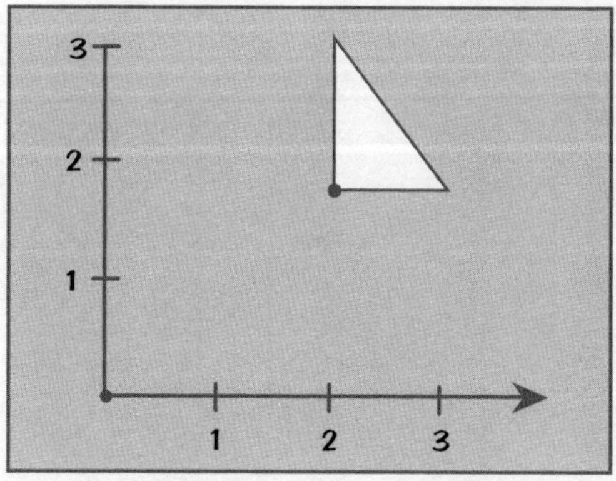

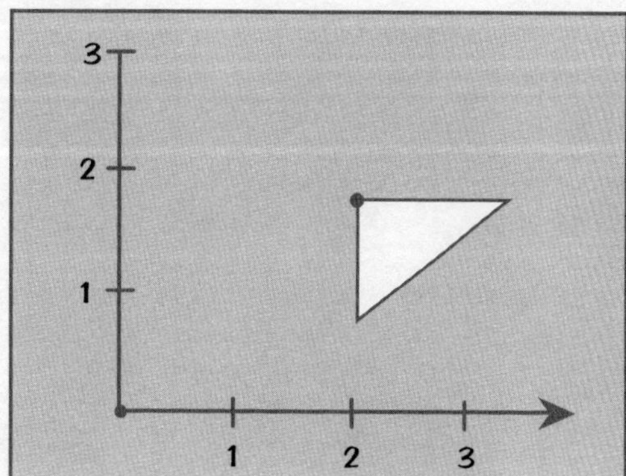

Rotation

Mathematics Assessment One

Responses *Throughout this section, pages from Mathematics Assessment One of the Student Workbook are included in reduced-page format. Correct multiple-choice answers and sample responses for each constructed-response item are indicated.*

Directions:

This Grade 6 Mathematics Assessment has multiple-choice and short-answer questions.

There are several important things to remember as you take this test:

- Read each multiple-choice question carefully. Think about what is being asked. Then fill in one answer bubble to mark your answer.
- If you do not know the answer to a multiple-choice question, skip it and go on. If you have time, go back to the questions you skipped and answer them.
- For short-answer questions, write your response clearly and neatly in the box provided.
- If you finish the Assessment early, go back and check over your work.

Mathematics Assessment One

Directions for Taking the Mathematics Assessment

The Mathematics Assessment is made up of multiple-choice and short-answer questions. These questions show you how the skills you have learned in Mathematics class may be tested. The questions also give you a chance to practice your skills. If you have trouble with an area, talk with a parent or teacher.

Multiple-choice questions require you to pick the best answer out of four possible choices. Only one answer is correct. The short-answer questions will ask you to write your answer and explain your thinking using words, numbers, or pictures, or to show the steps you used to solve a problem. Remember to read the questions and the answer choices carefully. You will mark your answers on the answer document.

When you finish, check your answers.

1. There are 30 students in Sara's class. Twelve of the students in her class are girls.

   What is the ratio of boys to girls?

   A. $\frac{12}{30}$

   B. $\frac{18}{30}$

   C. $\frac{12}{18}$

   ✗D. $\frac{18}{12}$

2. On Mrs. Booher's English exam, 4 students got As, 9 students got Bs, 15 students got Cs, and 2 students got Ds.

   What is the ratio of the B students to the number of students that took the exam?

   A. 1:2

   B. 3:7

   ✗C. 3:10

   D. 1:9

3. Kara wanted to buy breakfast cereal. She saw two brands at the store. Brand A costs \$4.48 for 16 ounces, and Brand B costs \$7.68 for 24 ounces.

   Which brand of cereal is the better buy?

   Show your work using words, numbers, or pictures.

   Brand A: \$4.48 ÷ 16 = \$0.28 per ounce

   Brand B: \$7.68 ÷ 24 = \$0.32 per ounce

   At \$0.28 per ounce, Brand A is the better buy because it costs less per ounce.

4. The ratio of boys to girls in Mr. Westbrook's History class is 4:5. In a class of 27 students, how many students are boys?

   A. 4

   B. about 4.5

   ✗C. 12

   D. 18

Go On

5. Look at the problem below.

   $$\frac{1}{3} \div \frac{3}{5}$$

   What is the correct answer to the division problem?

   A. $\frac{1}{5}$

   B. $\frac{5}{6}$

   ✗C. $\frac{5}{9}$

   D. $\frac{6}{9}$

6. There are 1,861 students at Genoa Middle School. Each classroom can seat 33 students.

   How many classrooms are needed to seat all the students?

   Show your work using words, numbers, or pictures.

   The school would need 57 classrooms to seat all the students in a classroom. The result of dividing 1,861 by 33 is 56 R13.

Go On

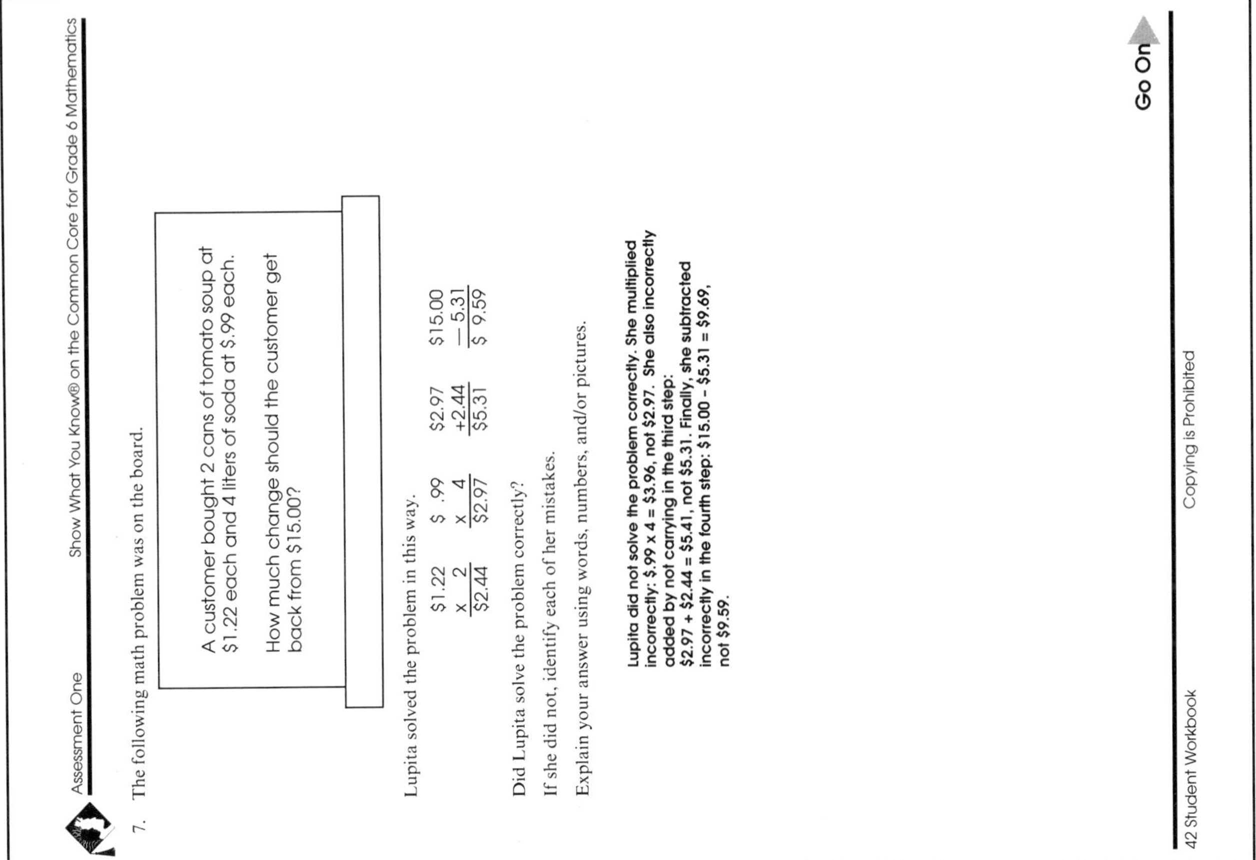

7. The following math problem was on the board.

> A customer bought 2 cans of tomato soup at $1.22 each and 4 liters of soda at $.99 each.
>
> How much change should the customer get back from $15.00?

Lupita solved the problem in this way.

$1.22	$ .99	$2.97	$15.00
x 2	x 4	+2.44	— 5.31
$2.44	$2.97	$5.31	$ 9.59

Did Lupita solve the problem correctly?

If she did not, identify each of her mistakes.

Explain your answer using words, numbers, and/or pictures.

Lupita did not solve the problem correctly. She multiplied incorrectly: $.99 x 4 = $3.96, not $2.97. She also incorrectly added by not carrying in the third step: $2.97 + $2.44 = $5.41, not $5.31. Finally, she subtracted incorrectly in the fourth step: $15.00 - $5.31 = $9.69, not $9.59.

Go On

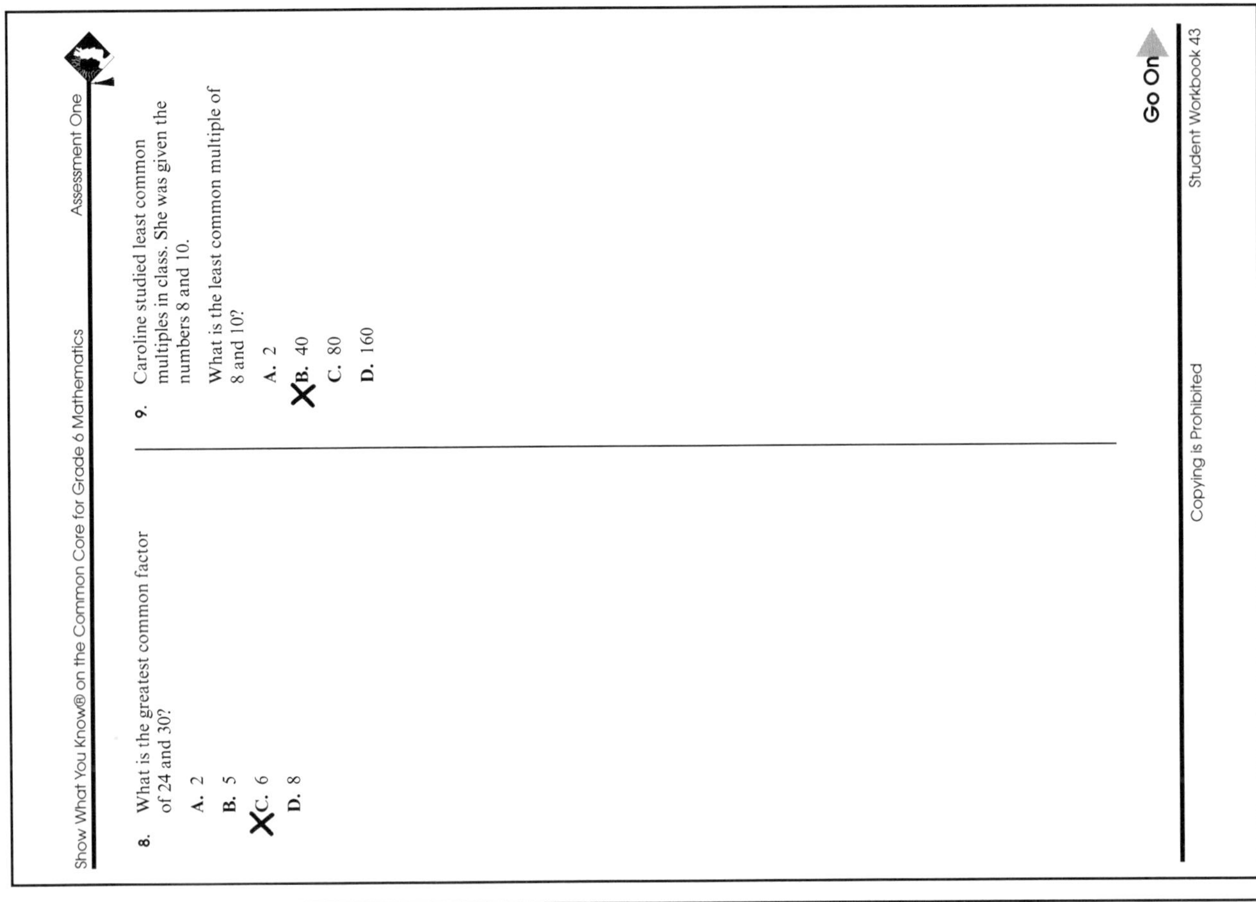

8. What is the greatest common factor of 24 and 30?

A. 2

B. 5

X **C.** 6

D. 8

9. Caroline studied least common multiples in class. She was given the numbers 8 and 10.

What is the least common multiple of 8 and 10?

A. 2

X **B.** 40

C. 80

D. 160

Go On

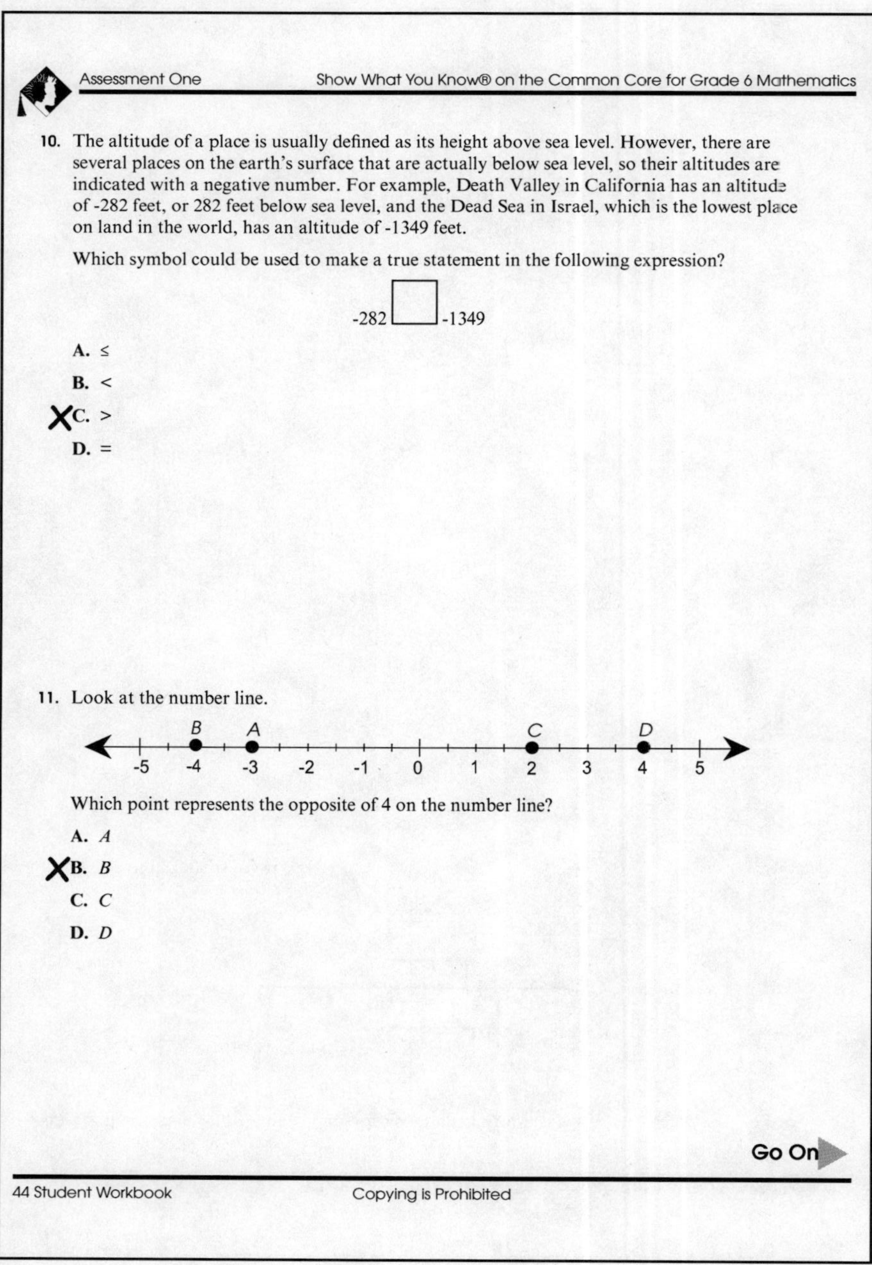

10. The altitude of a place is usually defined as its height above sea level. However, there are several places on the earth's surface that are actually below sea level, so their altitudes are indicated with a negative number. For example, Death Valley in California has an altitude of -282 feet, or 282 feet below sea level, and the Dead Sea in Israel, which is the lowest place on land in the world, has an altitude of -1349 feet.

Which symbol could be used to make a true statement in the following expression?

-282 ☐ -1349

A. ≤
B. <
X C. >
D. =

11. Look at the number line.

Which point represents the opposite of 4 on the number line?

A. *A*
X B. *B*
C. *C*
D. *D*

Go On

12. Which coordinate pair best represents Point *X* on the coordinate grid below?

A. (-3, 4)
B. (3, 4)
X C. (-4, 3)
D. (4, 3)

Go On

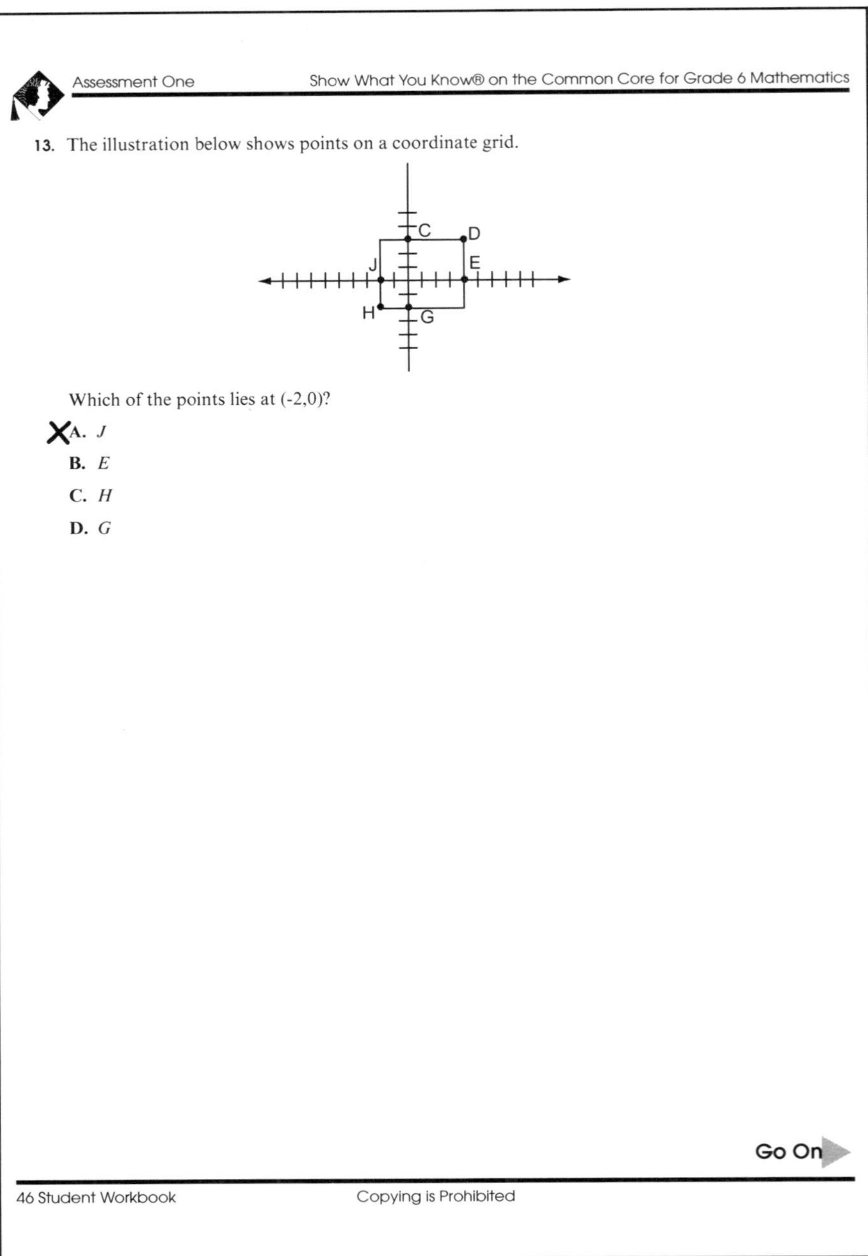

13. The illustration below shows points on a coordinate grid.

Which of the points lies at (-2,0)?

X **A.** *J*

B. *E*

C. *H*

D. *G*

Go On

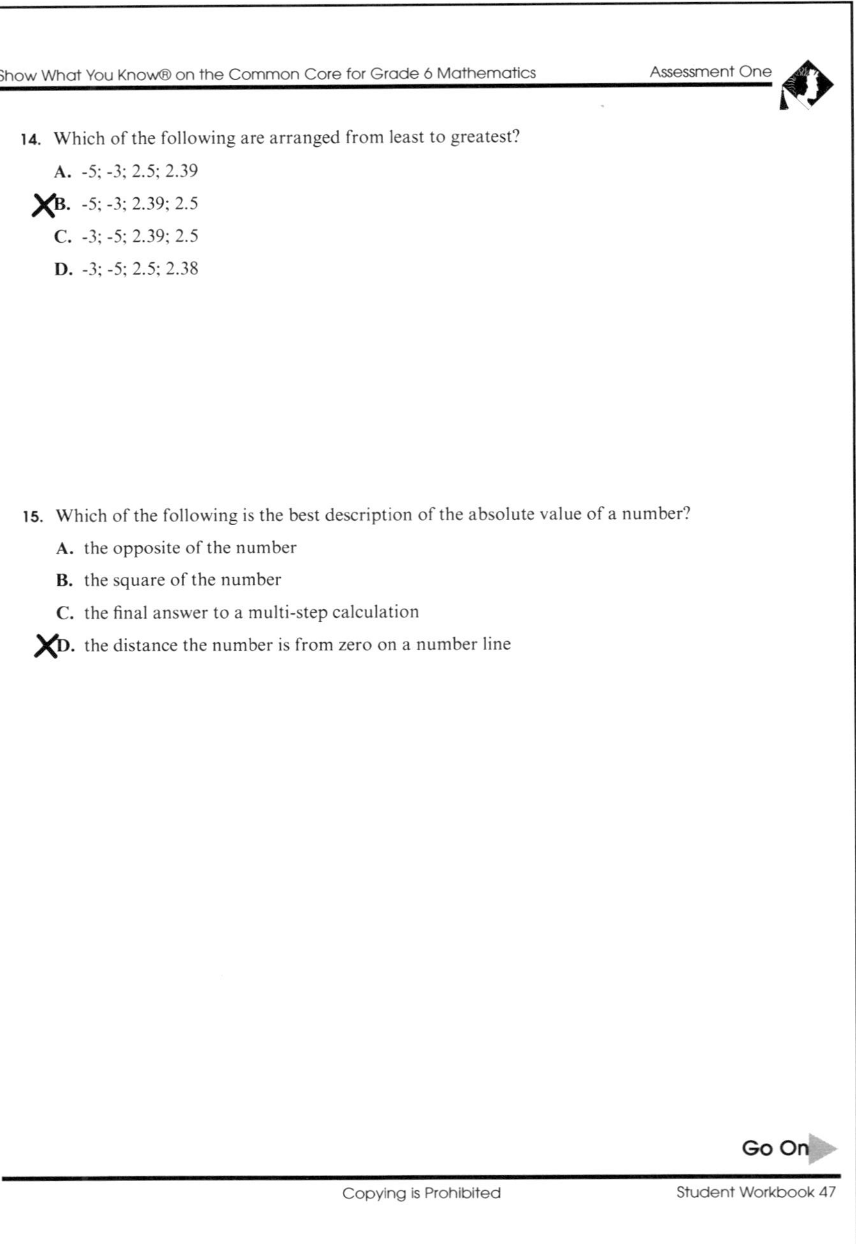

14. Which of the following are arranged from least to greatest?

A. -5; -3; 2.5; 2.39

X **B.** -5; -3; 2.39; 2.5

C. -3; -5; 2.39; 2.5

D. -3; -5; 2.5; 2.38

15. Which of the following is the best description of the absolute value of a number?

A. the opposite of the number

B. the square of the number

C. the final answer to a multi-step calculation

X **D.** the distance the number is from zero on a number line

Go On

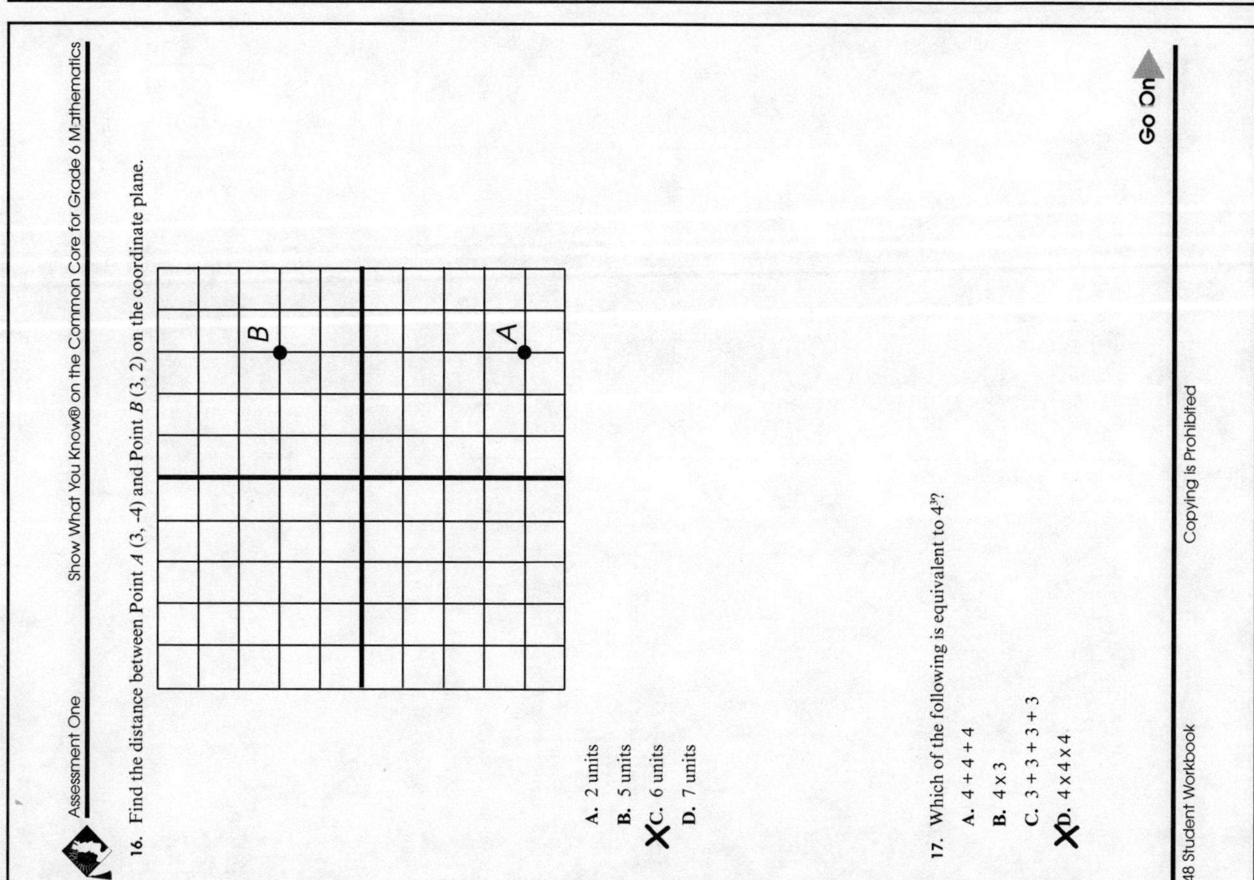

16. Find the distance between Point *A* (3, -4) and Point *B* (3, 2) on the coordinate plane.

A. 2 units

B. 5 units

X **C.** 6 units

D. 7 units

17. Which of the following is equivalent to 4^3?

A. 4 + 4 + 4

B. 4 x 3

C. 3 + 3 + 3 + 3

X **D.** 4 x 4 x 4

Go On

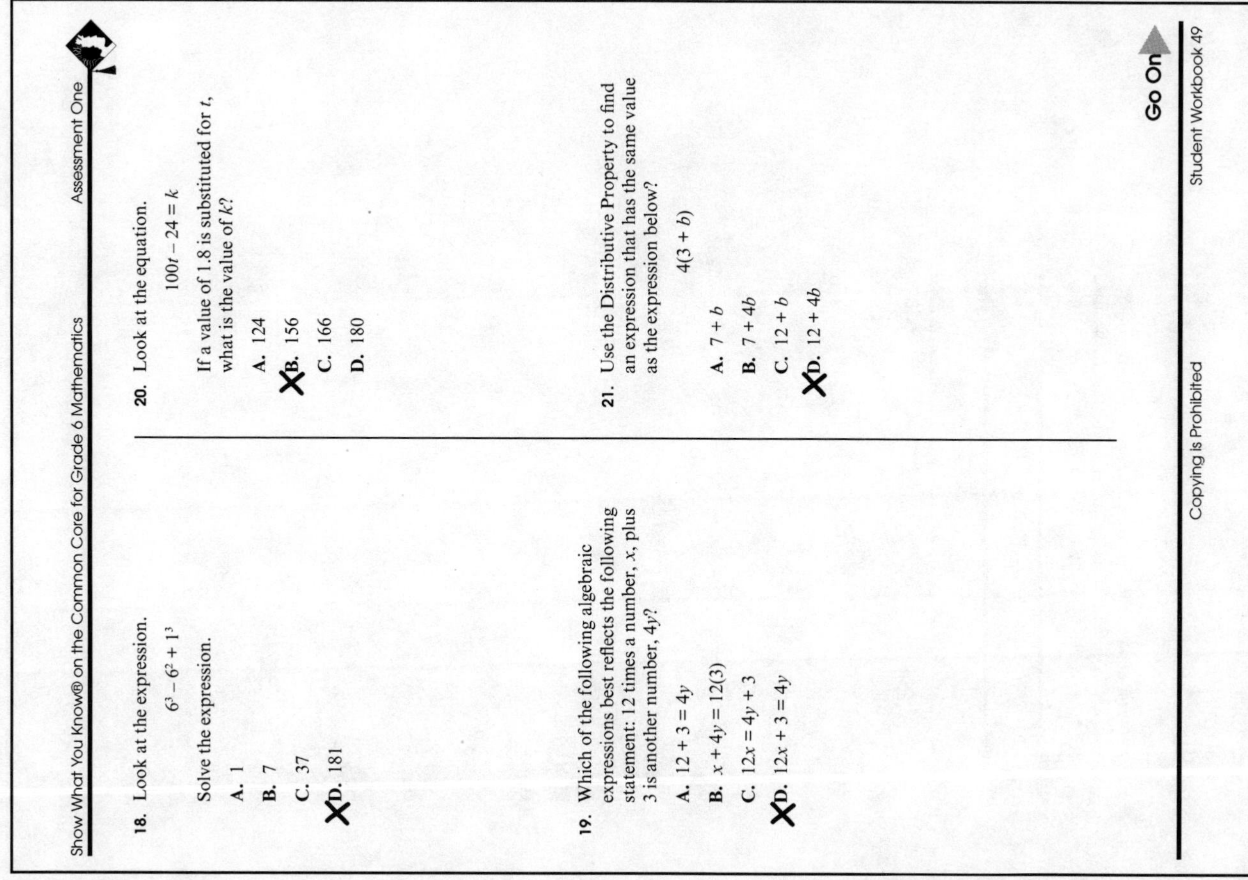

18. Look at the expression.

$$6^3 - 6^2 + 1^3$$

Solve the expression.

A. 1

B. 7

C. 37

X **D.** 181

19. Which of the following algebraic expressions best reflects the following statement: 12 times a number, *x*, plus 3 is another number, 4*y*?

A. $12 + 3 = 4y$

B. $x + 4y = 12(3)$

C. $12x = 4y + 3$

X **D.** $12x + 3 = 4y$

20. Look at the equation.

$$100t - 24 = k$$

If a value of 1.8 is substituted for *t*, what is the value of *k*?

A. 124

X **B.** 156

C. 166

D. 180

21. Use the Distributive Property to find an expression that has the same value as the expression below?

$$4(3 + b)$$

A. $7 + b$

B. $7 + 4b$

C. $12 + b$

X **D.** $12 + 4b$

Go On

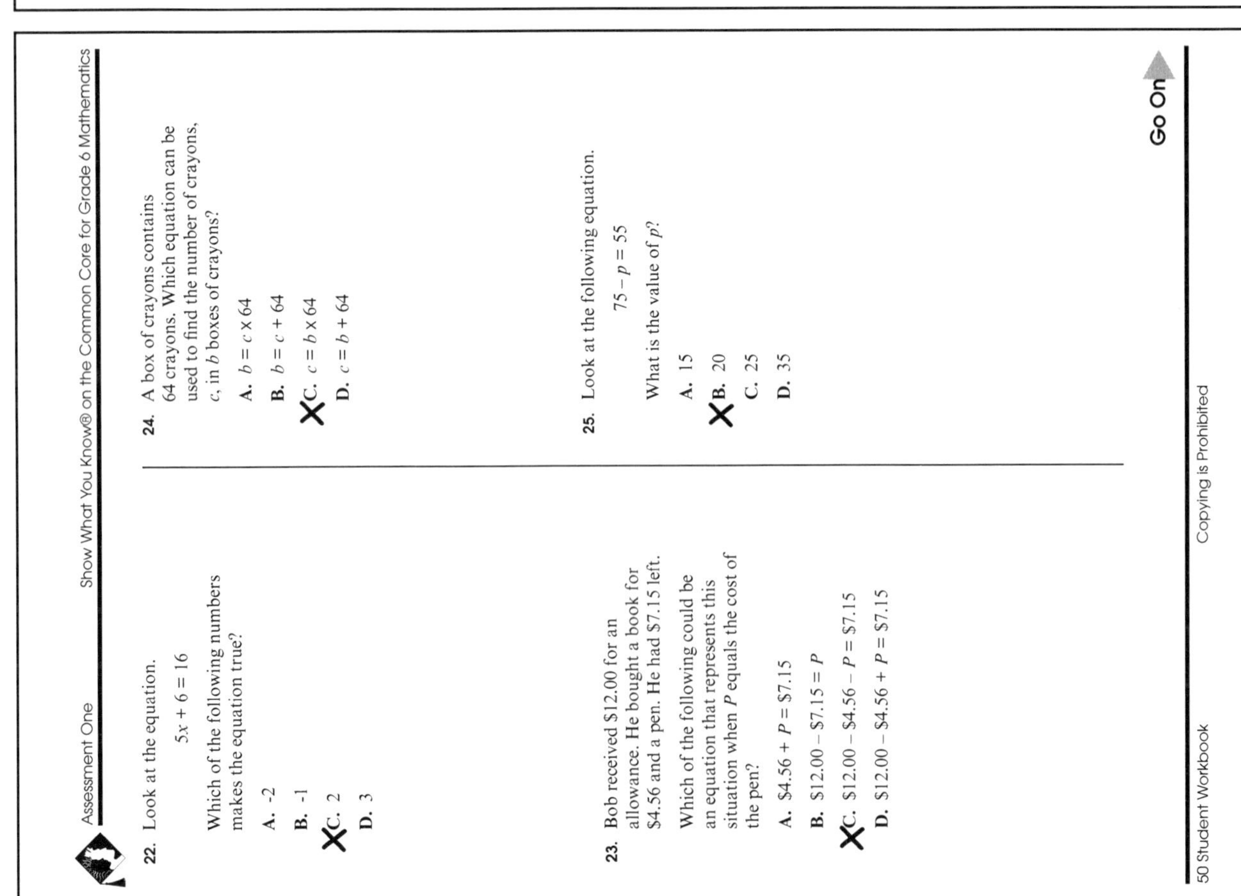

22. Look at the equation.

$5x + 6 = 16$

Which of the following numbers makes the equation true?

A. -2

B. -1

X **C.** 2

D. 3

23. Bob received $12.00 for an allowance. He bought a book for $4.56 and a pen. He had $7.15 left.

Which of the following could be an equation that represents this situation when *P* equals the cost of the pen?

A. $4.56 + *P* = $7.15

B. $12.00 – $7.15 = *P*

X **C.** $12.00 – $4.56 – *P* = $7.15

D. $12.00 – $4.56 + *P* = $7.15

24. A box of crayons contains 64 crayons. Which equation can be used to find the number of crayons, *c*, in *b* boxes of crayons?

A. $b = c \times 64$

B. $b = c + 64$

X **C.** $c = b \times 64$

D. $c = b + 64$

25. Look at the following equation.

$75 - p = 55$

What is the value of *p*?

A. 15

X **B.** 20

C. 25

D. 35

Go On

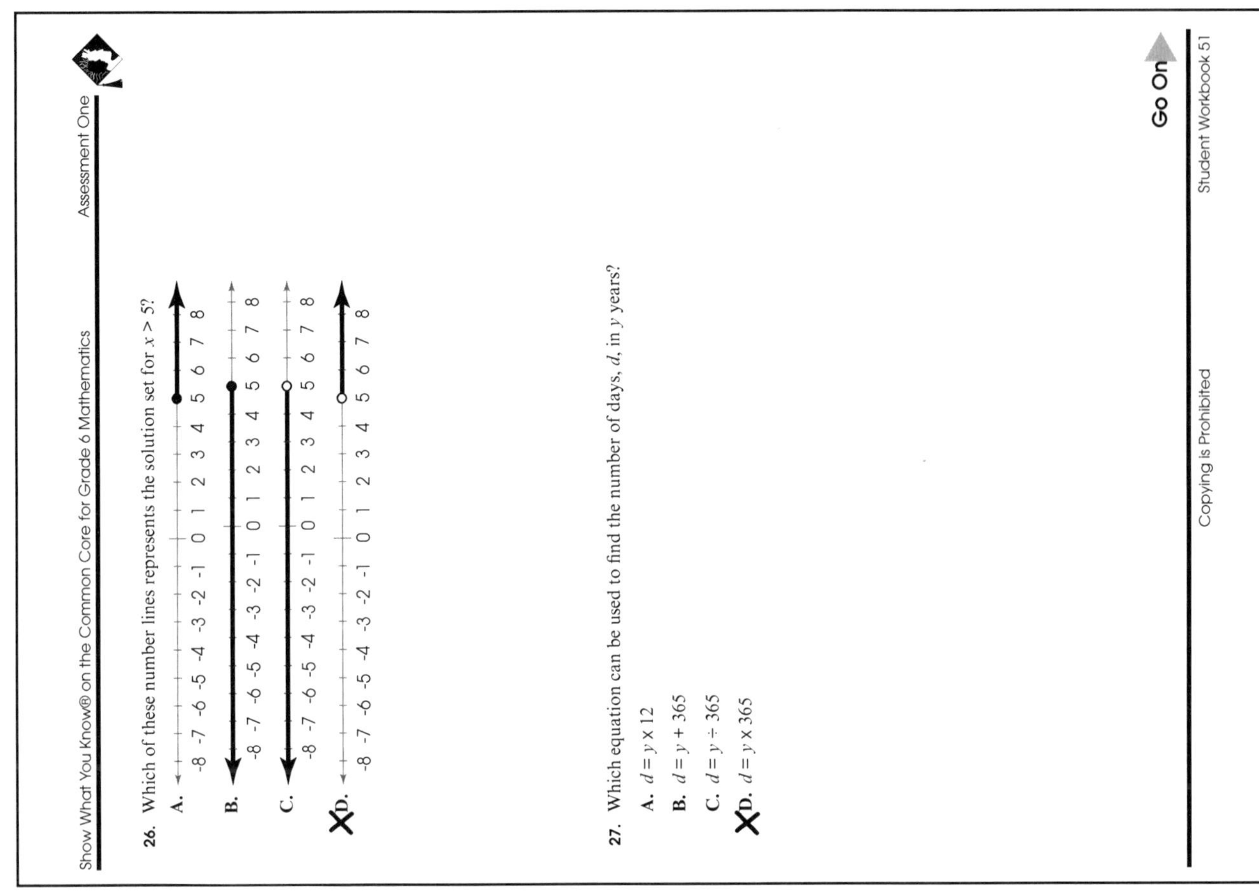

26. Which of these number lines represents the solution set for $x > 5$?

A. (number line from -8 to 8, closed circle at 5, arrow to the right)

B. (number line from -8 to 8, closed circle at 5, arrow to the left)

C. (number line from -8 to 8, open circle at 5, arrow to the left)

X **D.** (number line from -8 to 8, open circle at 5, arrow to the right)

27. Which equation can be used to find the number of days, *d*, in *y* years?

A. $d = y \times 12$

B. $d = y + 365$

C. $d = y \div 365$

X **D.** $d = y \times 365$

Go On

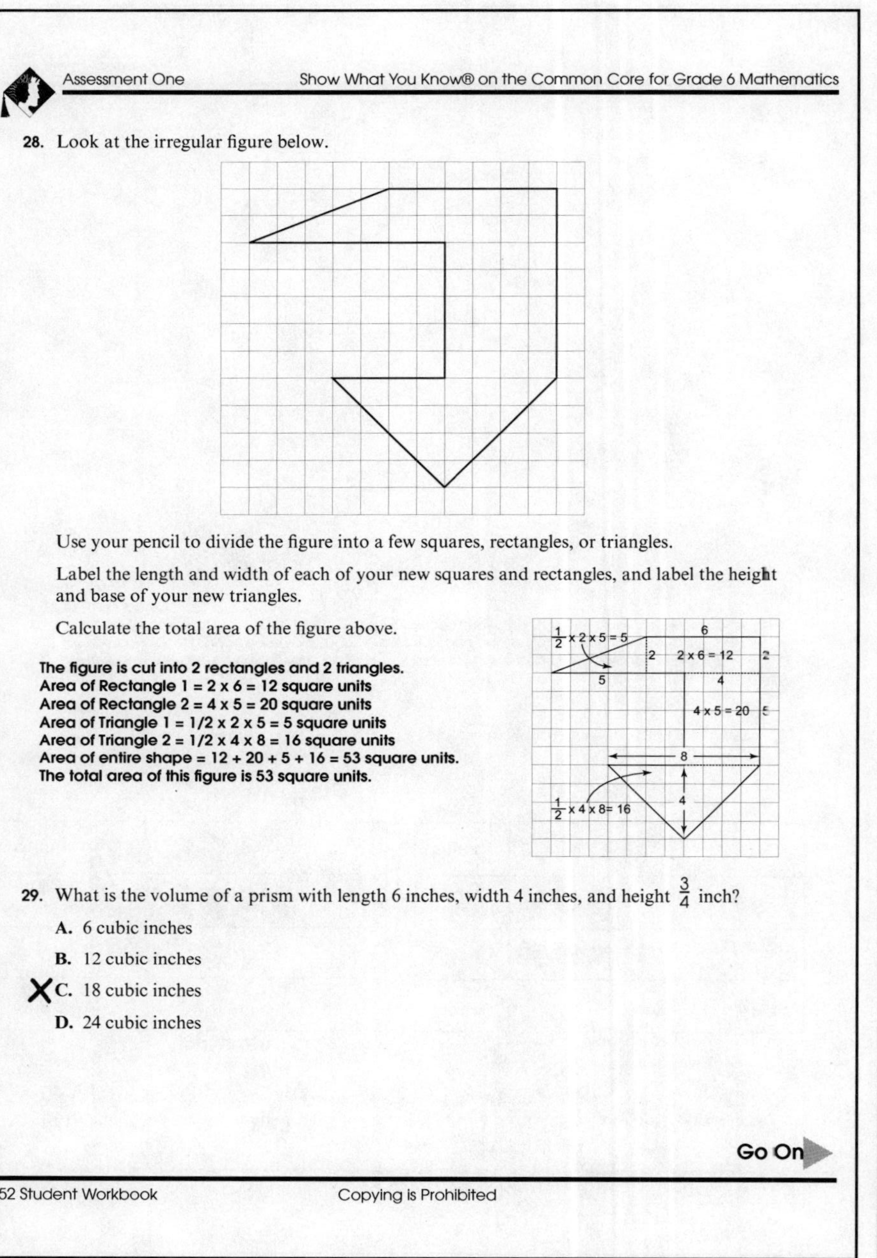

28. Look at the irregular figure below.

Use your pencil to divide the figure into a few squares, rectangles, or triangles.

Label the length and width of each of your new squares and rectangles, and label the height and base of your new triangles.

Calculate the total area of the figure above.

The figure is cut into 2 rectangles and 2 triangles.
Area of Rectangle 1 = 2 x 6 = 12 square units
Area of Rectangle 2 = 4 x 5 = 20 square units
Area of Triangle 1 = 1/2 x 2 x 5 = 5 square units
Area of Triangle 2 = 1/2 x 4 x 8 = 16 square units
Area of entire shape = 12 + 20 + 5 + 16 = 53 square units.
The total area of this figure is 53 square units.

29. What is the volume of a prism with length 6 inches, width 4 inches, and height $\frac{3}{4}$ inch?

A. 6 cubic inches
B. 12 cubic inches
X **C.** 18 cubic inches
D. 24 cubic inches

Go On

30. Which net correctly represents a cube?

A.

B.

C.

X **D.**

Go On

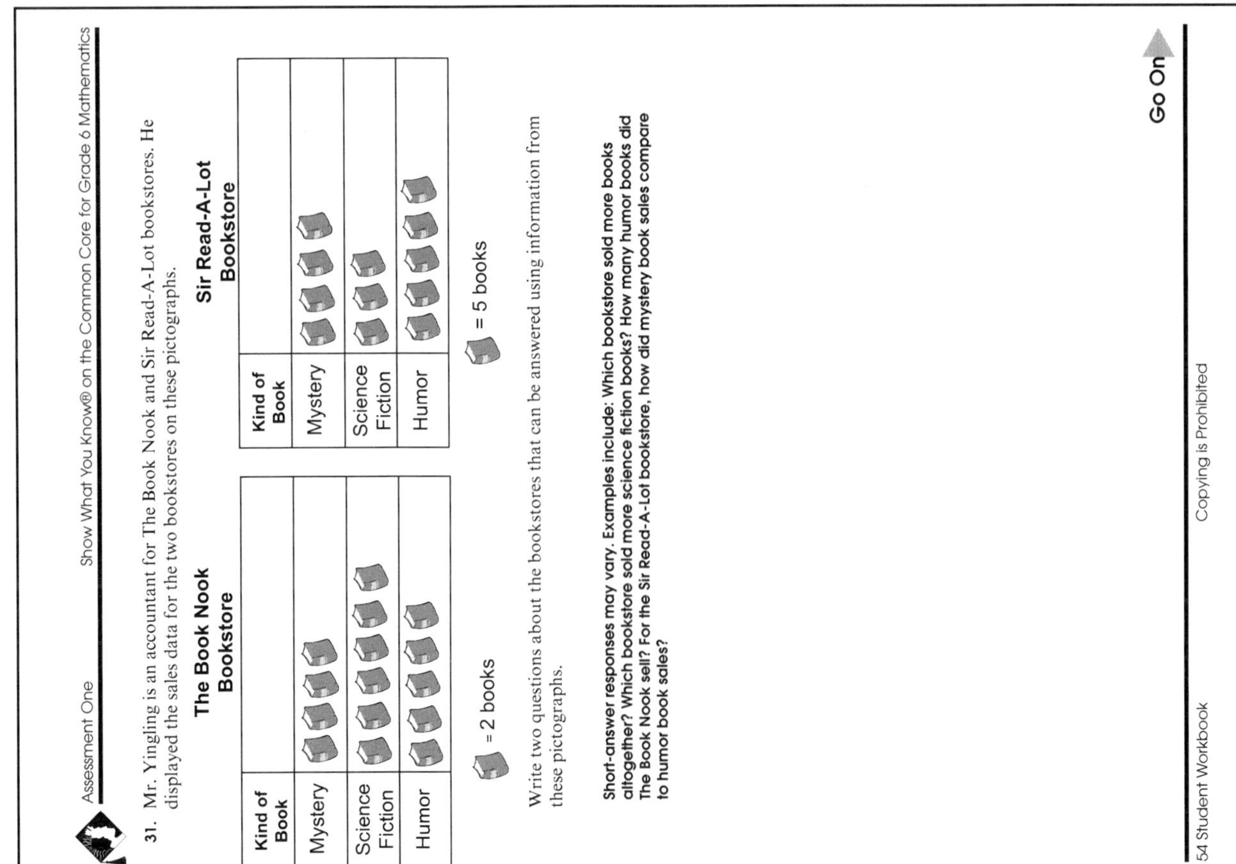

31. Mr. Yingling is an accountant for The Book Nook and Sir Read-A-Lot bookstores. He displayed the sales data for the two bookstores on these pictographs.

The Book Nook Bookstore

Kind of Book	
Mystery	4 book symbols
Science Fiction	6 book symbols
Humor	5 book symbols

= 2 books

Sir Read-A-Lot Bookstore

Kind of Book	
Mystery	4 book symbols
Science Fiction	3 book symbols
Humor	5 book symbols

= 5 books

Write two questions about the bookstores that can be answered using information from these pictographs.

Short-answer responses may vary. Examples include: Which bookstore sold more books altogether? Which bookstore sold more science fiction books? How many humor books did The Book Nook sell? For the Sir Read-A-Lot bookstore, how did mystery book sales compare to humor book sales?

Go On

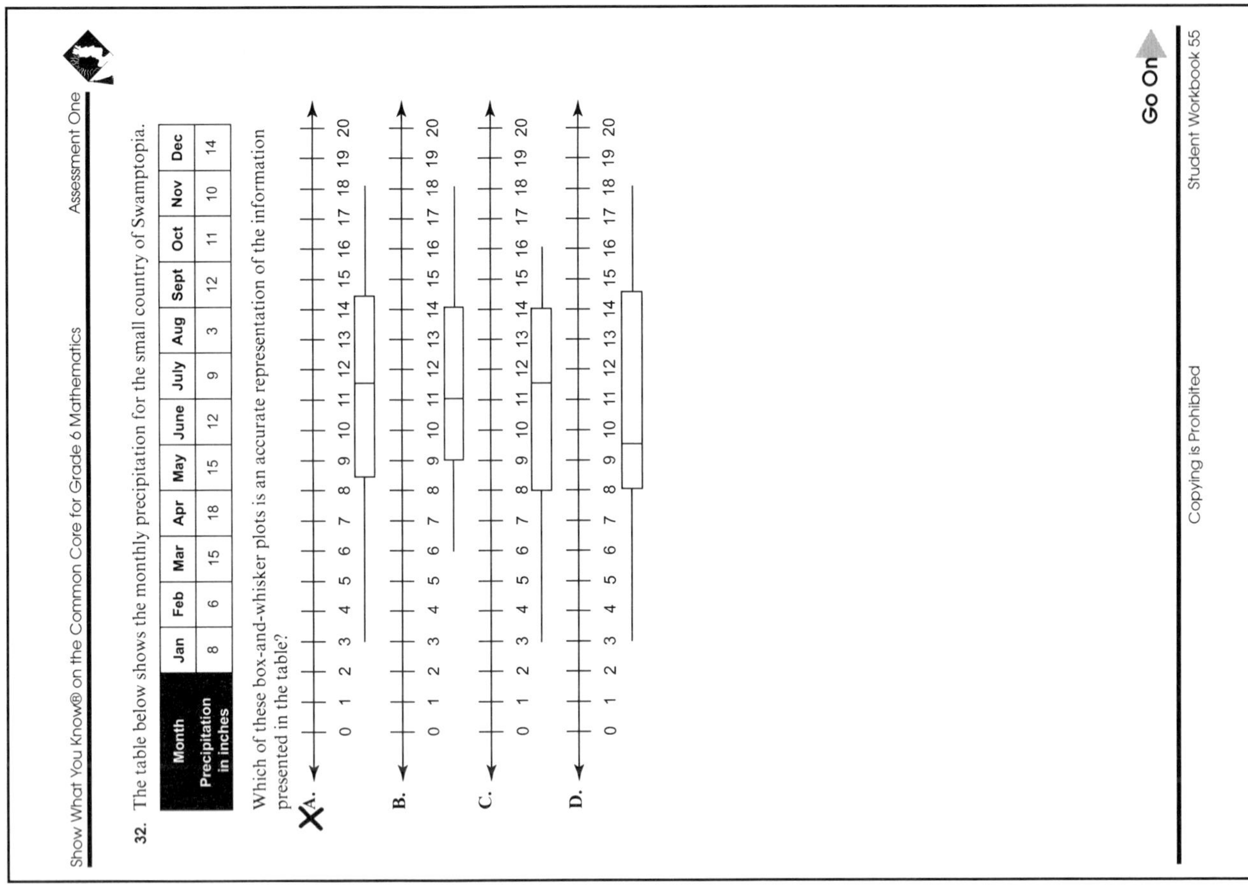

32. The table below shows the monthly precipitation for the small country of Swamptopia.

Month	Jan	Feb	Mar	Apr	May	June	July	Aug	Sept	Oct	Nov	Dec
Precipitation in inches	8	6	15	18	15	12	9	3	12	11	10	14

Which of these box-and-whisker plots is an accurate representation of the information presented in the table?

X A.
0 1 2 3 4 5 6 7 8 9 10 11 12 13 14 15 16 17 18 19 20

B.
0 1 2 3 4 5 6 7 8 9 10 11 12 13 14 15 16 17 18 19 20

C.
0 1 2 3 4 5 6 7 8 9 10 11 12 13 14 15 16 17 18 19 20

D.
0 1 2 3 4 5 6 7 8 9 10 11 12 13 14 15 16 17 18 19 20

Go On

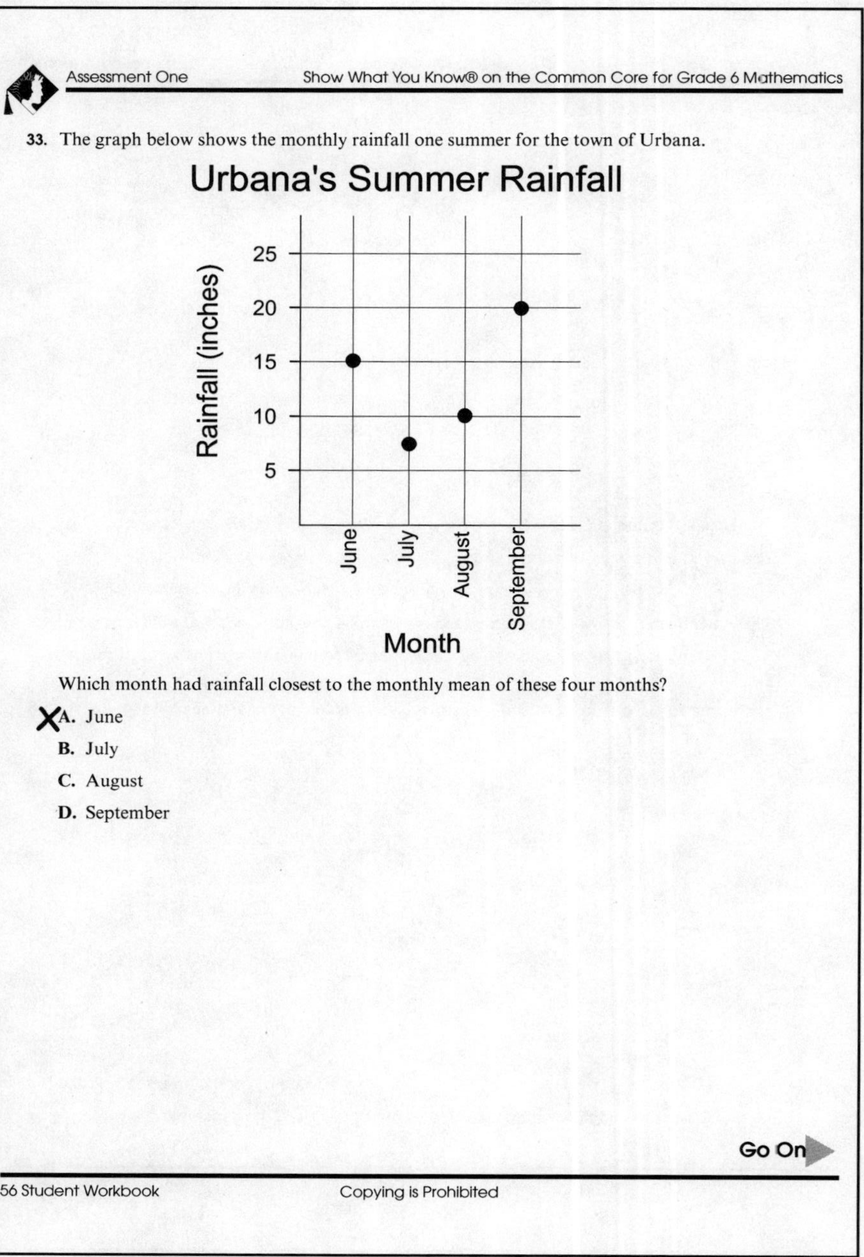

33. The graph below shows the monthly rainfall one summer for the town of Urbana.

Which month had rainfall closest to the monthly mean of these four months?

X A. June
B. July
C. August
D. September

Go On

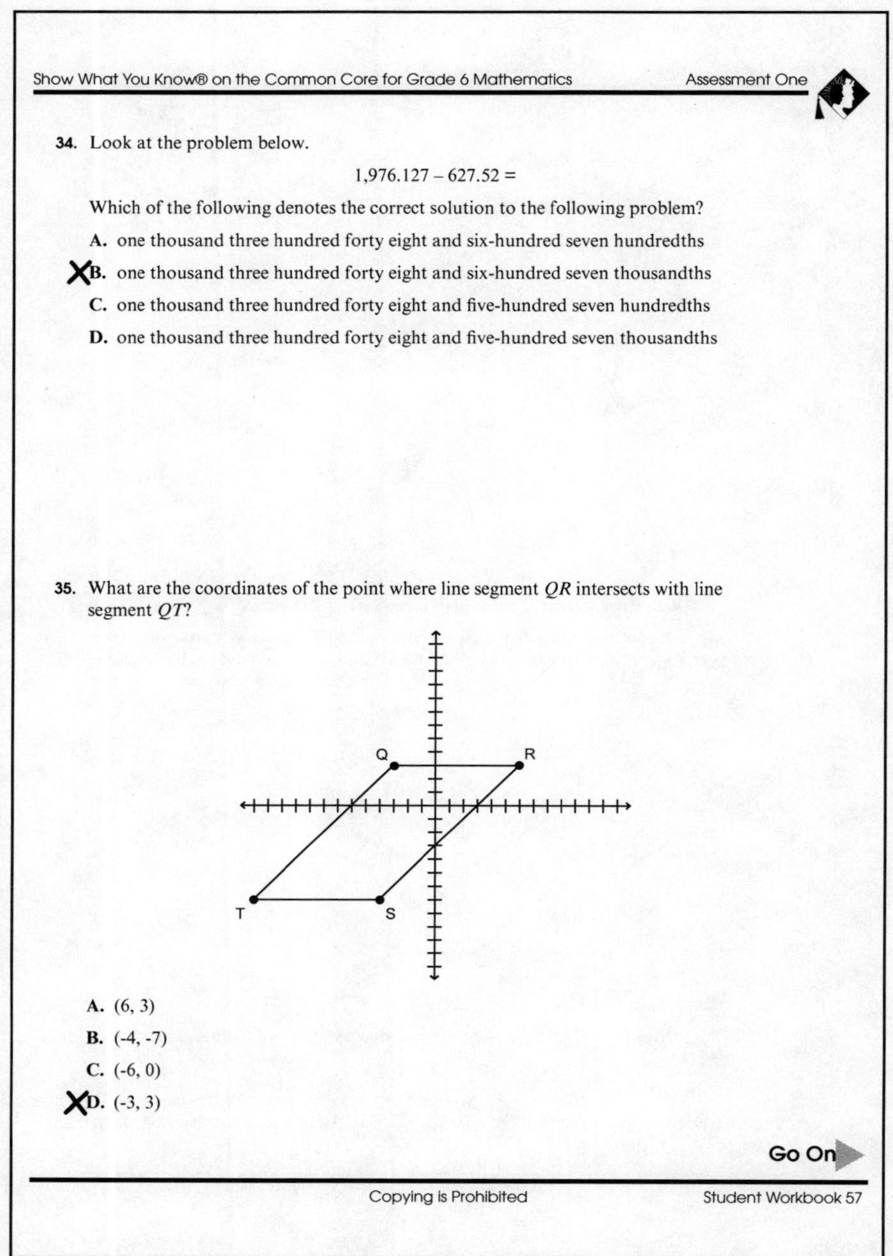

34. Look at the problem below.

$$1,976.127 - 627.52 =$$

Which of the following denotes the correct solution to the following problem?

A. one thousand three hundred forty eight and six-hundred seven hundredths
X B. one thousand three hundred forty eight and six-hundred seven thousandths
C. one thousand three hundred forty eight and five-hundred seven hundredths
D. one thousand three hundred forty eight and five-hundred seven thousandths

35. What are the coordinates of the point where line segment QR intersects with line segment QT?

A. (6, 3)
B. (-4, -7)
C. (-6, 0)
X D. (-3, 3)

Go On

36. There are 30 students in Sara's class. Eighteen of the students in her class are boys.

What is the ratio of girls to boys?

A. 12/30

B. 18/30

X**C.** 2/3

D. 18/12

37. Supersudz Laundry Detergent comes in two sizes. The large size contains 40 oz and costs $5.60. The super duper size has 64 oz and costs $7.04.

Which of these statements will help a shopper decide which box is the better buy?

A. The large size is the better buy because it is less expensive per ounce of detergent.

B. The large size is the better buy because $5.60 is less than $7.04.

C. The super duper size is a better buy because it is more expensive per ounce of detergent.

X**D.** The super duper size is a better buy because it is less expensive per ounce of detergent.

Go On

38. Kim plays basketball for her high school. During 1 month, she played 9 games. The number of points she scored in each game is listed below.

13, 7, 5, 11, 8, 7, 7, 10, 13

What is the median of the number of points she scored during these 9 games?

A. 3

B. 7

X**C.** 8

D. 9

39. Manny wants to put a fence around his garden to keep the rabbits out. He knows the perimeter is equal to $2l + 2w$ where l equals the length and the w equals the width.

If his garden is 16 feet long and 9 feet wide, what is the perimeter of the garden?

A. 25 ft.

X**B.** 50 ft.

C. 144 ft.

D. 288 ft.

Go On

40. Which method cannot be used to find the area of the trapezoid?

A. Divide the trapezoid into a rectangle and two triangles and apply the formulas for the area of a rectangle and the area of two triangles: $A = 3 \times 6 + 2(\frac{1}{2} \times 3 \times 3)$.

B. Divide the trapezoid into two triangles and apply the formula for the area of a triangle twice: so $A = \frac{1}{2} \times 3 \times 9 + \frac{1}{2} \times 3 \times 6$.

C. Cut off a triangular piece of the trapezoid, rotate it 180° to form a rectangle, and apply the formula for the area of a rectangle: $A = 3 \times 7.5$.

X**D.** Find the average of the two bases of the trapezoid and multiply that times the trapezoid's height: $(9 + 6) \div 2 = 7.5$; $A = 7.5 \times 4.24$.

1   Ⓐ Ⓑ Ⓒ ●

2  Ⓐ Ⓑ ● Ⓓ

3

Brand A: \$4.48 ÷ 16 = \$0.28 per ounce
Brand B: \$7.68 ÷ 24 = \$0.32 per ounce
At \$0.28 per ounce, Brand A is the better buy because it costs less per ounce.

4 Ⓐ Ⓑ ● Ⓓ

5 Ⓐ Ⓑ ● Ⓓ

6

The school would need 57 classrooms to seat all the students in a classroom. The result of dividing 1,861 by 33 is 56 R13.

7

Lupita did not solve the problem correctly. She multiplied incorrectly: \$.99 x 4 = \$3.96, not \$2.97. She also incorrectly added by not carrying in the third step: \$2.97 + \$2.44 = \$5.41, not \$5.31. Finally, she subtracted incorrectly in the fourth step: \$15.00 – \$5.31 = \$9.69, not \$9.59.

8 Ⓐ Ⓑ ● Ⓓ

9 Ⓐ ● Ⓒ Ⓓ

10 Ⓐ Ⓑ ● Ⓓ

11 Ⓐ ● Ⓒ Ⓓ

12 Ⓐ Ⓑ ● Ⓓ

13 ● Ⓑ Ⓒ Ⓓ

14 Ⓐ ● Ⓒ Ⓓ

15 Ⓐ Ⓑ Ⓒ ●

16 Ⓐ Ⓑ ● Ⓓ

17 Ⓐ Ⓑ Ⓒ ●

18 Ⓐ Ⓑ Ⓒ ●

19 Ⓐ Ⓑ Ⓒ ●

20 Ⓐ ● Ⓒ Ⓓ

21 Ⓐ Ⓑ Ⓒ ●

22 Ⓐ Ⓑ ● Ⓓ

23 Ⓐ Ⓑ ● Ⓓ

24 Ⓐ Ⓑ ● Ⓓ

25 Ⓐ ● Ⓒ Ⓓ

26 Ⓐ Ⓑ Ⓒ ●

27 Ⓐ Ⓑ Ⓒ ●

28

The figure is cut into 2 rectangles and 2 triangles.
Area of Rectangle 1 = 2 x 6 = 12 square units.
Area of Rectangle 2 = 4 x 5 = 20 square units.
Area of Triangle 1 = 1/2 x 2 x 5 = 5 square units.
Area of Triangle 2 = 1/2 x 4 x 8 = 16 square units.
Area of entire shape = 12 + 20 + 5 + 16 = 53 square units.
The total area of this figure is 53 square units.

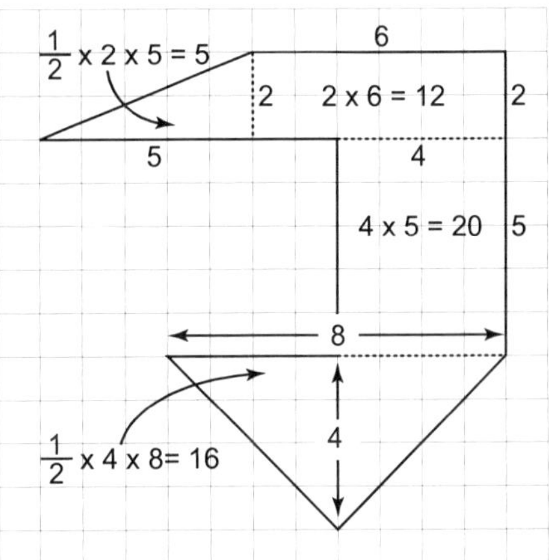

29 Ⓐ Ⓑ ● Ⓓ

30 Ⓐ Ⓑ Ⓒ ●

31

Short-answer responses may vary. Examples include: Which bookstore sold more books altogether? Which bookstore sold more science fiction books? How many humor books did The Book Nook sell? For the Sir Read-A-Lot bookstore, how did mystery book sales compare to humor book sales?

32 ● Ⓑ Ⓒ Ⓓ

33 ● Ⓑ Ⓒ Ⓓ

34 Ⓐ ● Ⓒ Ⓓ

35 Ⓐ Ⓑ Ⓒ ●

36 Ⓐ Ⓑ ● Ⓓ

37 Ⓐ Ⓑ Ⓒ ●

38 Ⓐ Ⓑ ● Ⓓ

39 Ⓐ ● Ⓒ Ⓓ

40 Ⓐ Ⓑ Ⓒ ●

Question	Standard	Answer	Keywords
1	6.RP.1	D	Ratio
2	6.RP.1	C	Ratio
3	6.RP.2	—	Unit Rate
4	6.RP.3	C	Ratio
5	6.NS.1	C	Division, Fractions
6	6.NS.2	—	Division
7	6.NS.3	—	Decimals
8	6.NS.4	C	Factors, Greatest Common Factor
9	6.NS.4	B	Multiples, Less Common Multiple
10	6.NS.5	C	Integers
11	6.NS.6	B	Integers, Opposites, Number Line
12	6.NS.6	C	Coordinate Plane, Graph, Coordinates
13	6.NS.6	A	Coordinate Plane, Graph, Coordinates
14	6.NS.7	B	Integers, Rational Numbers, Order
15	6.NS.7	D	Absolute Value
16	6.NS.8	C	Coordinate Plane, Distance
17	6.EE.1	D	Exponent, Numerical Expression
18	6.EE.1	D	Exponent, Evaluate
19	6.EE.2	D	Variable, Algebraic Expression, Translate
20	6.EE.2	B	Variable, Algebraic Expression, Evaluate

—see analysis for constructed response

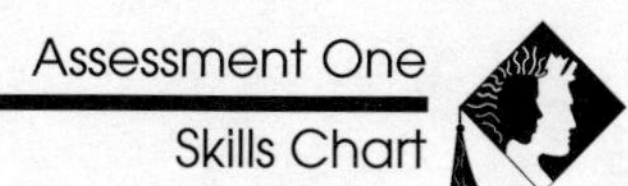

Question	Standard	Answer	Keywords
21	6.EE.3	D	Distributive Property, Equivalent Expressions
22	6.EE.5	C	Open Sentence, Equation, Solution Set
23	6.EE.6	C	Variable, Equation
24	6.EE.6	C	Variable, Equation
25	6.EE.7	B	Variable, Equation
26	6.EE.8	D	Inequality, Number Line
27	6.EE.9	D	Variables, Equations
28	6.G.1	—	Area, Irregular Figures
29	6.G.2	C	Volume, Rectangular Prism
30	6.G.4	D	Net, Rectangular Prism
31	6.SP.1	—	Statistics, Analyze Data
32	6.SP.4	A	Box-and-Whisker Plot, Display Data
33	6.SP.5	A	Mean
34	6.NS.3	B	Division, Decimal
35	6.NS.6	D	Coordinate Plane, Graph
36	6.RP.1	C	Ratio
37	6.RP.3	D	Unit Rate, Compare
38	6.SP.5	C	Median, Data
39	6.EE.2	B	Formula, Evaluate, Perimeter
40	6.G.1	D	Area, Trapezoid

—see analysis for constructed response

Mathematics Assessment One: Correlation Chart

Use this chart to identify areas for improvement for individual students or for the class as a whole. For example, enter students' names in the left-hand column. When a student misses a question, place an "X" in the corresponding box. A column with a large number of "Xs" shows that the class needs more practice with that particular objective.

Question	1	2	3	4	5	6	7	8	9	10	11	12	13	14	15	16	17	18	19	20
Answer	D	C	—	C	C	—	—	C	B	C	B	C	A	B	D	C	D	D	D	B
Correlation	6.RP.1	6.RP.1	6.RP.2	6.RP.3	6.NS.1	6.NS.2	6.NS.3	6.NS.4	6.NS.4	6.NS.5	6.NS.6	6.NS.6	6.NS.6	6.NS.7	6.NS.7	6.NS.8	6.EE.1	6.EE.1	6.EE.2	6.EE.2
Student Names																				

—see analysis for constructed response

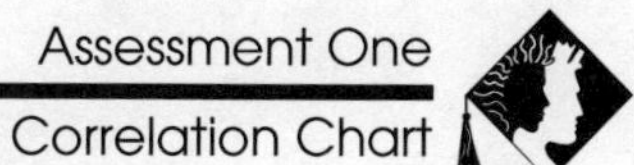

Correlation	6.EE.3	6.EE.5	6.EE.6	6.EE.6	6.EE.7	6.EE.8	6.EE.9	6.G.1	6.G.2	6.G.4	6.SP.1	6.SP.4	6.SP.5	6.NS.3	6.NS.6	6.RP.1	6.RP.3	6.SP.5	6.EE.2	6.G.1
Answer	D	C	C	C	B	D	D	—	C	D	—	A	A	B	D	C	D	C	B	D
Question	21	22	23	24	25	26	27	28	29	30	31	32	33	34	35	36	37	38	39	40
Student Names																				

—see analysis for constructed response

This page intentionally left blank.

Mathematics Assessment Two

Responses *Throughout this section, pages from Mathematics Assessment Two of the Student Workbook are included in reduced-page format. Correct multiple-choice answers and sample responses for each constructed-response item are indicated.*

Directions:

This Grade 6 Mathematics Assessment has multiple-choice and short-answer questions.

There are several important things to remember as you take this test:

- Read each multiple-choice question carefully. Think about what is being asked. Then fill in one answer bubble to mark your answer.
- If you do not know the answer to a multiple-choice question, skip it and go on. If you have time, go back to the questions you skipped and answer them.
- For short-answer questions, write your response clearly and neatly in the box provided.
- If you finish the Assessment early, go back and check over your work.

Mathematics Assessment Two

Directions for Taking the Mathematics Assessment

The Mathematics Assessment is made up of multiple-choice and short-answer questions. These questions show you how the skills you have learned in Mathematics class may be tested. The questions also give you a chance to practice your skills. If you have trouble with an area, talk with a parent or teacher.

Multiple-choice questions require you to pick the best answer out of four possible choices. Only one answer is correct. The short-answer questions will ask you to write your answer and explain your thinking using words, numbers, or pictures, or to show the steps you used to solve a problem. Remember to read the questions and the answer choices carefully. You will mark your answers on the answer document.

When you finish, check your answers.

1. For his birthday, Pedro took 63 cookies to share with his class.

   If there are a total of 21 students in the class, what is the ratio of cookies to students?

   ✗ **A.** 3 to 1
   B. 1 to 3
   C. 7 to 1
   D. 1 to 7

2. Ali's Fruit Market makes fruit baskets for their customers. In their premium fruit baskets, they pack 4 grapefruit, 6 pears, 10 tangerines, 4 oranges, and 12 plums.

   What is the ratio of pears to other types of fruit?

   A. 1/6
   ✗ **B.** 1/5
   C. 1/3
   D. 6

3. Choco-Bombs Breakfast Cereal comes in 32-ounce boxes and costs $2.40. Big Sugar Bits comes in 20-ounce boxes and costs $1.64.

   Which of these is the better buy?

   Show how you got your answer using words, numbers, or pictures.

   The unit-rate cost of the Choco-Bombs is 7 1/2¢ ($0.075) per ounce. The unit-rate cost of the Big Sugar Bits is 8.2¢ ($0.082) per ounce. Since the Choco-Bombs cost less per ounce, they would be the better buy.

4. Theo went to his garden to pick apples from his apple tree. Of the 60 apples he counted on the tree, only 20% were ripe.

   If Theo picked only the ripe apples from the tree, how many apples did Theo pick?

   A. 3 apples
   B. 5 apples
   ✗ **C.** 12 apples
   D. 20 apples

Go On

5. Look at the problem below.

   $$\frac{1}{3} \div \frac{3}{4}$$

   What is the answer to the division problem?

   A. $\frac{1}{4}$
   B. $\frac{4}{6}$
   ✗ **C.** $\frac{4}{9}$
   D. $\frac{5}{9}$

6. Michelle wants to know the average number of miles she drives using one gallon of gasoline. She knows that she has driven 3,626 miles using 98 gallons of gasoline. She divides 3,626 by 98 to find the average number of miles per gallon. Her result is 47.

   Use estimation to decide if Michelle's result is correct.

   Show how you got your answer using words, numbers, or pictures.

   Michelle's result is incorrect. The quotient can be estimated by rounding the number of miles driven to 3,600 and the number of gallons of gasoline used to 100. Dividing 3,600 by 100 results in an estimated average number of miles per gallon of 36. Michelle's result is too large to be correct. The correct answer is 37 miles per gallon.

7. Robby's sister must mail out 120 wedding invitations. Each invitation will require $.60 postage. Stamps are available in the following denominations: $.01, $.05, $.19, $.39, and $.45. Robby volunteered to go to the post office to pick up the stamps.

   Is there a way to get exactly $.60 postage for each invitation?

   How much money will Robby need to buy the stamps?

   Show your work using words, numbers, and/or pictures.

   There are several ways to get exactly 60 cents in postage from the denominations above. Here are three examples:
   a. one 45-cent stamp and three 5-cent stamps (45 + 3 x 5 = 45 + 15 = 60)
   b. three 19-cent stamps and three 1-cent stamps (3 x 19 + 3 x 1 = 57 + 3 = 60)
   c. one 39-cent stamp, four 5-cent stamps, and one 1-cent stamp (39 + 4 x 5 + 1 = 39 + 20 + 1 = 60)
   When Robby goes to the post office, he will need $72.00 to buy the stamps. (120 x $.60 = $72.00)

8. What is the greatest common factor of 48 and 72?

   A. 4
   B. 8
   C. 12
   ✗ **D.** 24

Go On

9. What is the least common multiple of 6 and 12?

A. 6
✗B. 12
C. 24
D. 72

10. Gordon owes money on a second mortgage bank loan. The loan is set up so that he can use as much money as he wants, up to a pre-set limit of $40,000. Gordon notices that his loan balance always appears as a positive number on his statement. Payments he makes to the loan always appear on the statement with a "-" before them.

In a mathematical sense, which of the following best explains this situation?

A. A mistake has been made since loan amounts must be "negative," and there would be no way to credit a payment if the balance is shown as "positive."
✗B. If a loan can be stated as a "positive" amount, then payments would need to be subtracted from the balance owed to keep an accurate tally.
C. His loan balance isn't positive or negative, but the amount he could still borrow up to the $40,000 limit must be "negative."
D. His loan balance isn't positive or negative, but the amount he could still borrow up to the $40,000 limit must be "positive."

Go On

11. Which point represents the opposite of –2 on the number line below?

C (-5), B (-2), D (2), A (3)
-5 -4 -3 -2 -1 0 1 2 3 4 5

A. *A*
B. *B*
C. *C*
✗D. *D*

Go On

12. At what coordinate is Point S located on the grid below?

X A. (2, -1)
B. (-1, -2)
C. (-1, 2)
D. (2, 1)

Go On

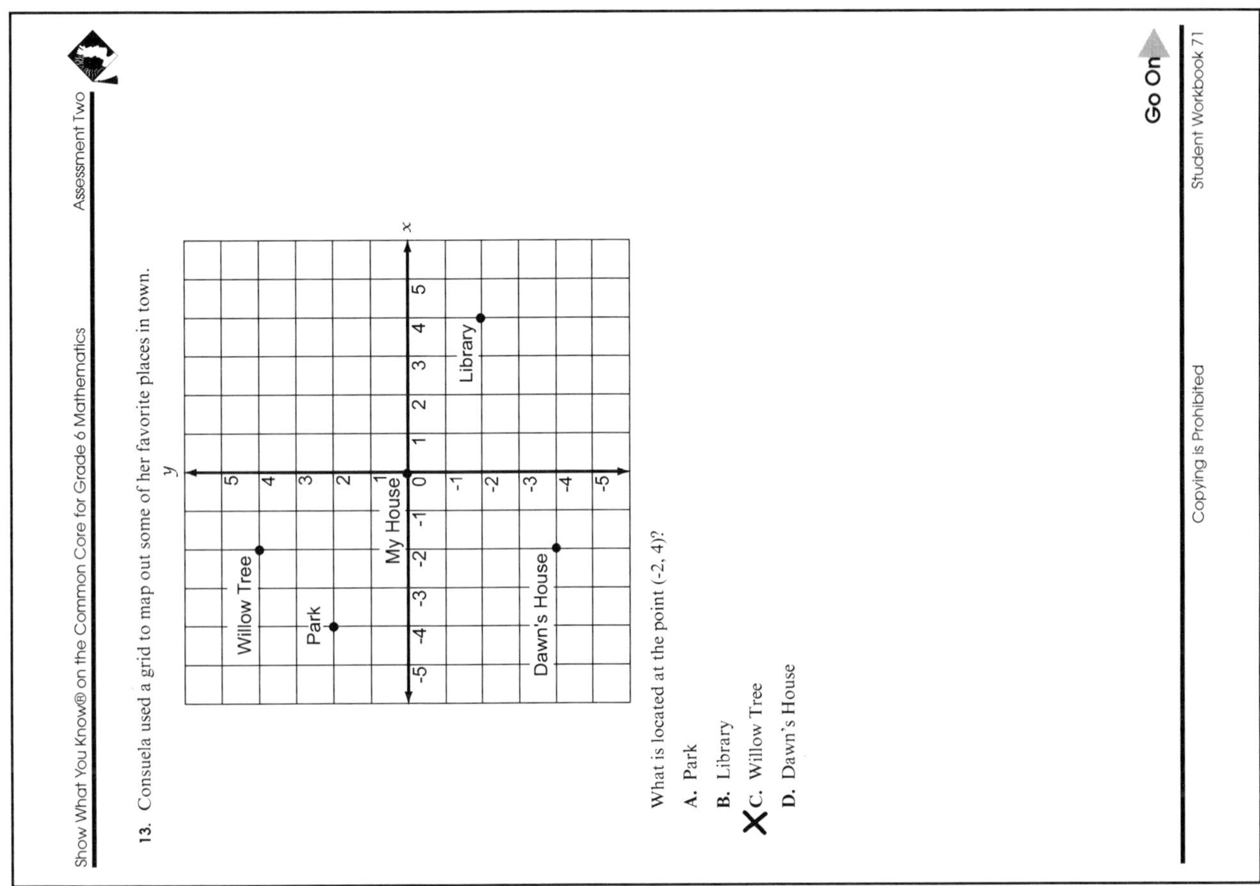

13. Consuela used a grid to map out some of her favorite places in town.

What is located at the point (-2, 4)?

A. Park
B. Library
X C. Willow Tree
D. Dawn's House

Go On

14. Which of the following is less than -3?

A. $2\frac{1}{2}$

B. 0

C. -1

X**D.** -5

15. Look at the expression.

|-15| ____ |12|

Choose the correct symbol to complete the expression.

A. ≤

B. <

X**C.** >

D. =

16. Find the distance between $A(-2, 4)$ and $B(5, 4)$ on the coordinate plane.

A. 1 unit

B. 3 units

C. 6 units

X**D.** 7 units

17. What is another way of writing 4^2?

A. 4 x 2

B. 4 + 2

X**C.** 4 x 4

D. 4 + 4

Go On

18. Which of the following expressions is true?

A. $2^5 = 2 \times 5$

B. $3^3 = 9$

C. $2^7 = 2 \times 2 \times 2 \times 2 \times 2 \times 2 \times 2 = 512$

X**D.** $2^3 \times 3^2 \times 5 \times 7 = 2{,}520$

19. Read the following statement.

The product of a number and seven decreased by two is twelve.

Which expression correctly represents this statement?

A. $(x \div 7) - 2 = 12$

X**B.** $7x - 2 = 12$

C. $(7 + x) - 2 = 12$

D. $7x \div 2 = 12$

20. Look at the expression.

$5(x - 3)$

What is the value of the expression when $x = 7$?

A. 7

X**B.** 20

C. 32

D. 35

21. Use the Distributive Property to find an expression that has the same value as the expression below?

$18a + 12b$

X**A.** $6(3a + 2b)$

B. $6(2a + 3b)$

C. $2(9a + 8b)$

D. $3(3a + 4b)$

Go On

22. Look at the equation.

$$4x + 3 = 15$$

Which number makes the equation true?

A. -2

B. -1

C. 2

X **D.** 3

23. Four wheels are needed for each toy car.

Which of the following would be a simple equation to determine total number of wheels, W, needed for any number of toy cars made, C?

A. $W = 4 + C$

B. $C = 4 + W$

X **C.** $W = 4C$

D. $C = 4W$

24. Howard is 5 years younger than his older sister Kathryn.

If h represents Howard's age, which of the following expressions could be used to find Kathryn's age?

A. $h \times 5$

B. $h \div 5$

C. $h - 5$

X **D.** $h + 5$

25. Look at the equation.

$$1.6x = 12.8$$

Solve the one-step equation.

A. 0.8

X **B.** 8

C. 11.2

D. 20.48

Go On

26. Tom wants to find a summer job that pays at least $5 per hour.

Which of the choices below correctly graphs the statement "at least $5 per hour?"

A. -8 -7 -6 -5 -4 -3 -2 -1 0 1 2 3 4 5 6 7 8

X **B.** -8 -7 -6 -5 -4 -3 -2 -1 0 1 2 3 4 5 6 7 8

C. -8 -7 -6 -5 -4 -3 -2 -1 0 1 2 3 4 5 6 7 8

D. -8 -7 -6 -5 -4 -3 -2 -1 0 1 2 3 4 5 6 7 8

27. At a movie theater, the price of admission is $7.50.

Write a formula to determine how much money (m) was taken in for admission, where t stands for the number of tickets sold.

The amount of money (*m*) taken in is equal to the number of tickets sold multiplied by the price of each ticket, so the formula is *m* = $7.50 x *t* or m = $7.50*t*.

Go On

28. Look at the irregular quadrilateral below.

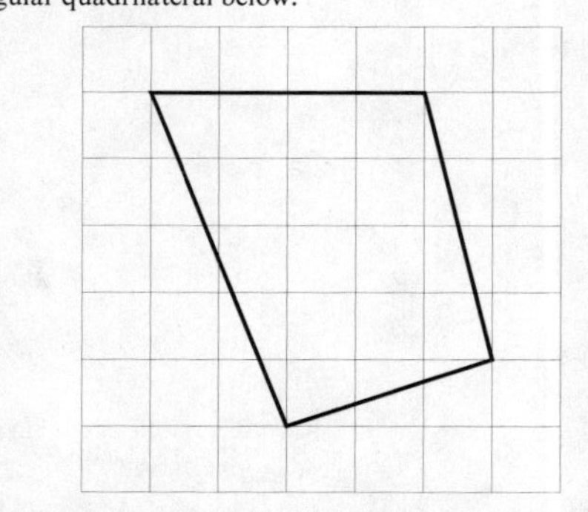

What is the approximate area of the irregular quadrilateral?

X **A.** 16.5 square units

B. 17.5 square units

C. 20 square units

D. 25 square units

29. What is the volume of a prism with length 8 inches, width 3 inches, and height $\frac{2}{3}$ inch?

A. 8 cubic inches

B. 12 cubic inches

X **C.** 16 cubic inches

D. 24 cubic inches

Go On

30. Ana is using a coordinate grid to draw a quadrilateral. She selected four points:

F (-3, 1)

G (-3, 3)

H (2, 8)

I (5, 9).

Place the ordered pairs listed above and label them *F*, *G*, *H*, and *I*.

Use a straight edge to connect the four points to make a quadrilateral.

What type of quadrilateral is formed?

Describe the attributes of the figure.

The quadrilateral is a trapezoid. Two sides of the quadrilateral, GH and FI, are parallel, which means they also have the same slope.

31. The measures of center—mean, median, and mode—are used to describe data involving a single variable, that is, univariate data.

Which of the following is NOT an example of univariate data?

A. beginning teachers' salaries

B. classmates' exam scores

C. heights of a random group of men

X **D.** students' grades on a test and the number of days until their next birthday

Go On

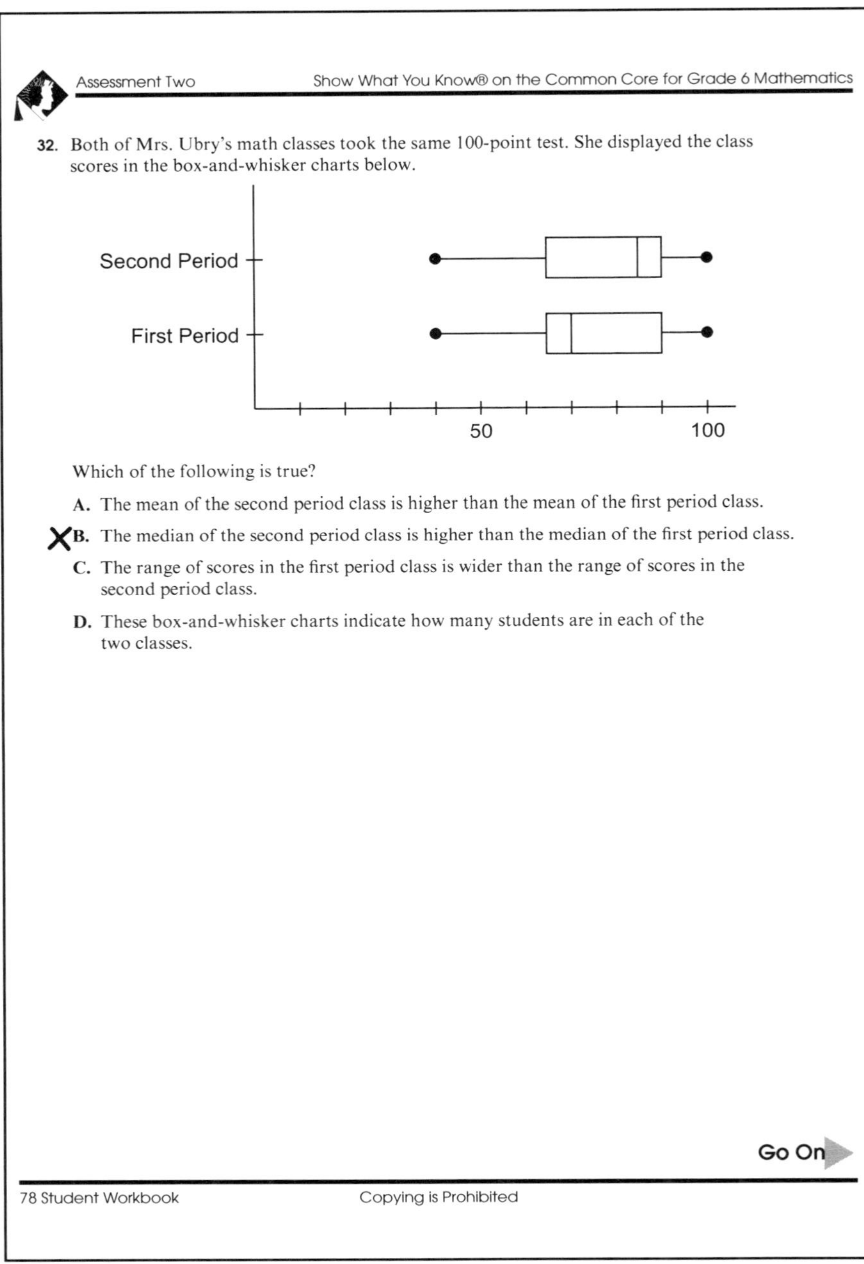

32. Both of Mrs. Ubry's math classes took the same 100-point test. She displayed the class scores in the box-and-whisker charts below.

Which of the following is true?

A. The mean of the second period class is higher than the mean of the first period class.

X B. The median of the second period class is higher than the median of the first period class.

C. The range of scores in the first period class is wider than the range of scores in the second period class.

D. These box-and-whisker charts indicate how many students are in each of the two classes.

Go On

33. The histogram shown below shows all students' scores on an algebra exam.

[Histogram — y-axis: 0, 10, 20, 30, 40, 50; x-axis: 10, 20, 30, 40, 50, 60, 70, 80, 90, 100]

In which interval does the median fall?

A. 60–70

X B. 70–80

C. 80–90

D. 90–100

Go On

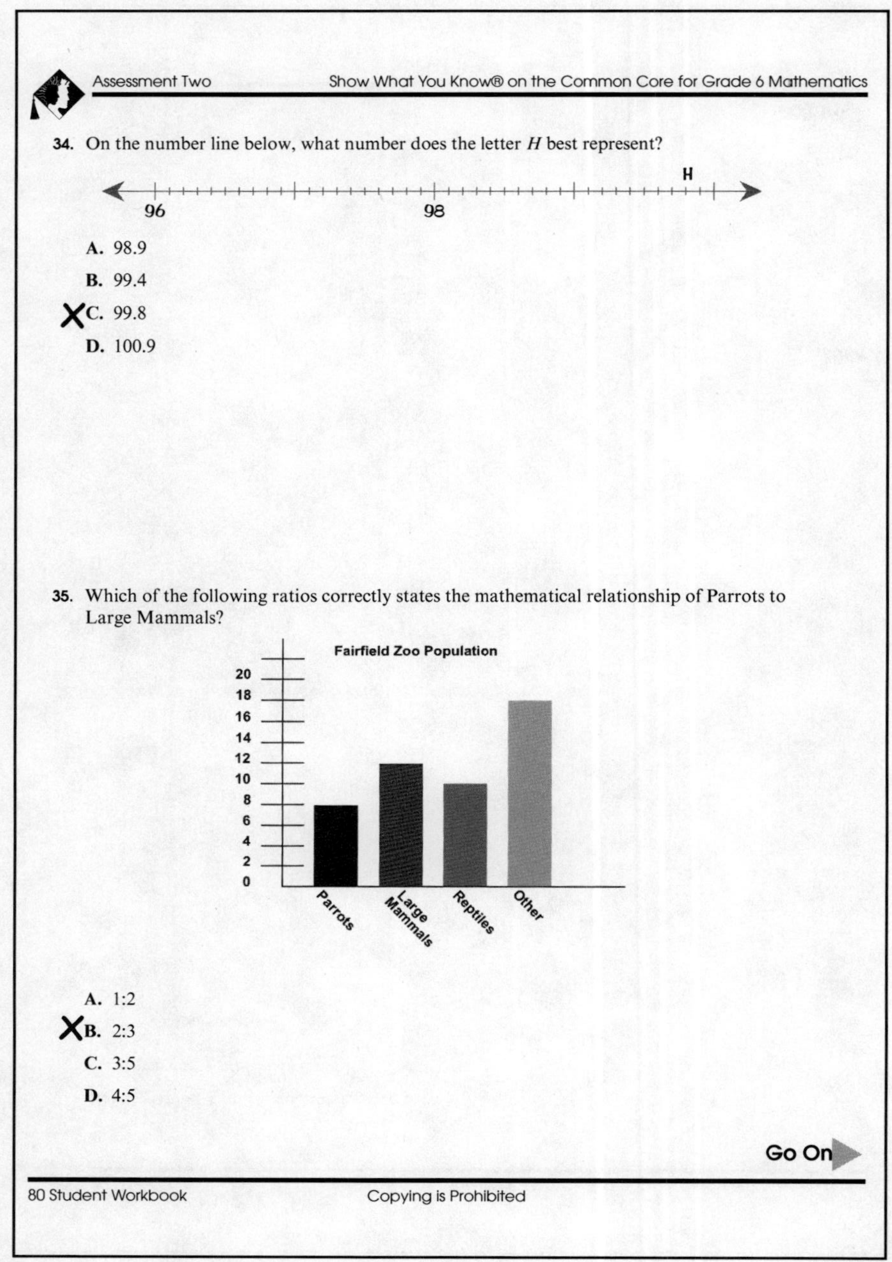

34. On the number line below, what number does the letter H best represent?

A. 98.9

B. 99.4

X **C.** 99.8

D. 100.9

35. Which of the following ratios correctly states the mathematical relationship of Parrots to Large Mammals?

A. 1:2

X **B.** 2:3

C. 3:5

D. 4:5

Go On

36. The graph below shows the number of boys and girls in each sixth grade teacher's class at Toth Elementary School.

Number of students
16
12
8
4
Mr. Rava
Mrs. Moffett
Mr. Hrivnyak
Teachers
= boys
= girls

What is the mean number of girls in these three classes?

A. 8

B. 12

X **C.** 14

D. 42

Go On

37. Collin planted $\frac{3}{5}$ of his vegetable garden.

What percent is left to be planted?

A. 20%

B. 30%

X C. 40%

D. 60%

38. Which of the following choices correctly represents the expression 5^3?

A. 5 x 3

X B. 5 x 5 x 5

C. 3 x 3 x 3

D. 5 + 5 + 5

Go On

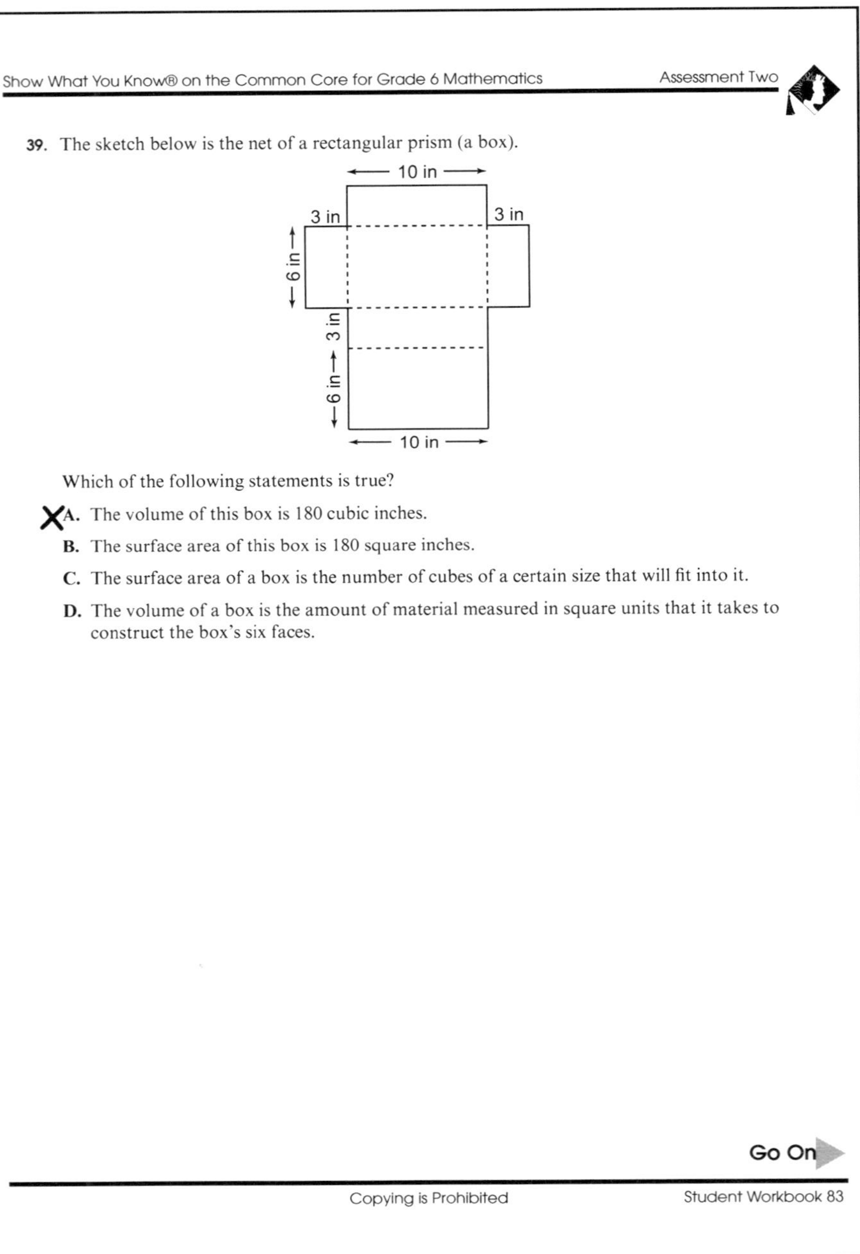

39. The sketch below is the net of a rectangular prism (a box).

Which of the following statements is true?

X A. The volume of this box is 180 cubic inches.

B. The surface area of this box is 180 square inches.

C. The surface area of a box is the number of cubes of a certain size that will fit into it.

D. The volume of a box is the amount of material measured in square units that it takes to construct the box's six faces.

Go On

40. The hot dog stand charges \$1.75 for a basic hot dog and \$0.85 for a drink. The "special" includes a hot dog, a drink, and a bag of chips. The special costs only a nickel more than the hot dog and drink alone.

Which of the following is a simplified expression that would figure the total purchase amount regardless of the number of specials, *S*, purchased?

A. (\$1.75)*S* + (\$ 0.85)

B. (\$1.75)*S* + (\$ 0.85)*S* + (\$ 0.05)

C. (\$2.60)*S*

X **D.** (\$2.65)*S*

STOP

1 ● Ⓑ Ⓒ Ⓓ

2 Ⓐ ● Ⓒ Ⓓ

3

The cereal that is the better buy is Choco-Bombs.

The unit-rate cost of the Choco-Bombs is 7 1/2¢ ($0.075) per ounce. The unit-rate cost of the Big Sugar Bits is 8.2¢ ($0.082) per ounce. Since the Choco-Bombs cost less per ounce, they would be the better buy.

4 Ⓐ Ⓑ ● Ⓓ

5 Ⓐ Ⓑ ● Ⓓ

6

Michelle's result is incorrect. The quotient can be estimated by rounding the number of miles driven to 3,600 and the number of gallons of gasoline used to 100. Dividing 3,600 by 100 results in an estimated average number of miles per gallon of 36. Michelle's result is too large to be correct. The correct answer is 37 miles per gallon.

7

There are several ways to get exactly 60 cents in postage from the denominations above. Here are three examples:
a. one 45-cent stamp and three 5-cent stamps
(45 + 3 x 5 = 45 + 15 = 60)
b. three 19-cent stamps and three 1-cent stamps
(3 x 19 + 3 x 1 = 57 + 3 = 60)
c. one 39-cent stamp, four 5-cent stamps, and one 1-cent stamp
(39 + 4 x 5 + 1 = 39 + 20 + 1 = 60) When Robby goes to the post office, he will need $72.00 to buy the stamps.
(120 x $.60 = $72.00)

8 Ⓐ Ⓑ Ⓒ ●
9 Ⓐ ● Ⓒ Ⓓ
10 Ⓐ ● Ⓒ Ⓓ
11 Ⓐ Ⓑ Ⓒ ●
12 ● Ⓑ Ⓒ Ⓓ
13 Ⓐ Ⓑ ● Ⓓ
14 Ⓐ Ⓑ Ⓒ ●
15 Ⓐ Ⓑ ● Ⓓ
16 Ⓐ Ⓑ Ⓒ ●
17 Ⓐ Ⓑ ● Ⓓ
18 Ⓐ Ⓑ Ⓒ ●
19 Ⓐ ● Ⓒ Ⓓ
20 Ⓐ ● Ⓒ Ⓓ
21 ● Ⓑ Ⓒ Ⓓ
22 Ⓐ Ⓑ Ⓒ ●
23 Ⓐ Ⓑ ● Ⓓ

24 Ⓐ Ⓑ Ⓒ ●

25 Ⓐ ● Ⓒ Ⓓ

26 Ⓐ ● Ⓒ Ⓓ

27

$m = \$7.50t$

The amount of money (m) taken in is equal to the number of tickets sold multiplied by the price of each ticket, so the formula is $m = \$7.50 \times t$ or $m = \$7.50t$.

28 ● Ⓑ Ⓒ Ⓓ

29 Ⓐ Ⓑ ● Ⓓ

30

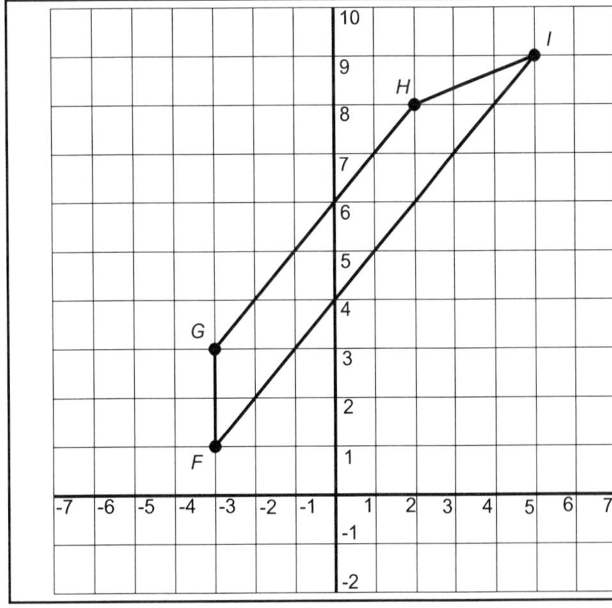

The quadrilateral is a trapezoid. Two sides of the quadrilateral, *GH* and *FI*, are parallel, which means they also have the same slope.

31 Ⓐ Ⓑ Ⓒ ●
32 Ⓐ ● Ⓒ Ⓓ
33 Ⓐ ● Ⓒ Ⓓ
34 Ⓐ Ⓑ ● Ⓓ
35 Ⓐ ● Ⓒ Ⓓ
36 Ⓐ Ⓑ ● Ⓓ
37 Ⓐ Ⓑ ● Ⓓ
38 Ⓐ ● Ⓒ Ⓓ
39 ● Ⓑ Ⓒ Ⓓ
40 Ⓐ Ⓑ Ⓒ ●

Question	Standard	Answer	Keywords
1	6.RP.1	A	Ratio
2	6.RP.1	B	Ratio
3	6.RP.2	—	Unit Rate
4	6.RP.3	C	Ratio
5	6.NS.1	C	Division, Fractions
6	6.NS.2	—	Division, Estimation
7	6.NS.3	—	Decimals
8	6.NS.4	D	Factors, Greatest Common Factor
9	6.NS.4	B	Multiples, Less Common Multiple
10	6.NS.5	B	Integers, Mathematical Sense
11	6.NS.6	D	Integers, Opposites, Number Line
12	6.NS.6	A	Coordinate Plane, Graph, Coordinates
13	6.NS.6	C	Coordinate Plane, Graph, Coordinates
14	6.NS.7	D	Integers, Rational Numbers, Compare
15	6.NS.7	C	Absolute Value
16	6.NS.8	D	Coordinate Plane, Distance
17	6.EE.1	C	Exponent, Numerical Expression
18	6.EE.1	D	Exponents, Evaluate
19	6.EE.2	B	Variable, Algebraic Expression, Translate
20	6.EE.2	B	Variable, Algebraic Expression, Evaluate

—see analysis for constructed response

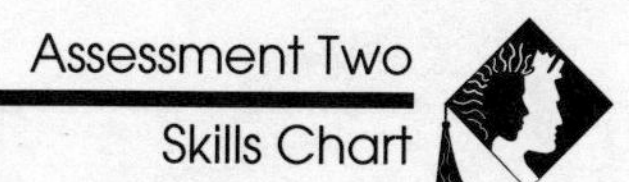

Question	Standard	Answer	Keywords
21	6.EE.3	A	Distributive Property, Equivalent Expressions
22	6.EE.5	D	Open Sentence, Equation, Solution Set
23	6.EE.6	C	Variable, Equation
24	6.EE.6	D	Variable, Equation
25	6.EE.7	B	Variable, Equation
26	6.EE.8	B	Inequality, Number Line
27	6.EE.9	—	Variables, Equations
28	6.G.1	A	Area, Irregular Figures
29	6.G.2	C	Volume, Rectangular Prism
30	6.G.3	—	Coordinate Grid, Graph, Trapezoid
31	6.SP.3	D	Univariate Data
32	6.SP.2	B	Box-and-Whisker Plot, Display Data
33	6.SP.5	B	Histogram, Median
34	6.NS.6	C	Number Line, Decimal
35	6.Rp.1	B	Ratio
36	6.SP.5	C	Mean, Data
37	6.RP.3	C	Percent
38	6.EE.1	B	Exponent
39	6.G.4	A	Net, Rectangular Prism, Volume
40	6.EE.4	D	Expression, Simplify

—see analysis for constructed response

Mathematics Assessment Two: Correlation Chart

Use this chart to identify areas for improvement for individual students or for the class as a whole. For example, enter students' names in the left-hand column. When a student misses a question, place an "X" in the corresponding box. A column with a large number of "Xs" shows that the class needs more practice with that particular objective.

Question	1	2	3	4	5	6	7	8	9	10	11	12	13	14	15	16	17	18	19	20
Answer	A	B	—	C	C	—	—	D	B	B	D	A	C	D	C	D	C	D	B	B
Correlation	6.RP.1	6.RP.1	6.RP.2	6.RP.3	6.NS.1	6.NS.2	6.NS.3	6.NS.4	6.NS.4	6.NS.5	6.NS.6	6.NS.6	6.NS.6	6.NS.7	6.NS.7	6.NS.8	6.EE.1	6.EE.1	6.EE.2	6.EE.2
Student Names																				

—*see analysis for constructed response*

Question	21	22	23	24	25	26	27	28	29	30	31	32	33	34	35	36	37	38	39	40
Answer	A	D	C	D	B	B	—	A	C	—	D	B	B	C	B	C	C	B	A	D
Correlation	6.EE.3	6.EE.5	6.EE.6	6.EE.6	6.EE.7	6.EE.8	6.EE.9	6.G.1	6.G.2	6.G.3	6.SP.3	6.SP.2	6.SP.5	6.NS.6	6.RP.1	6.SP.5	6.RP.3	6.EE.1	6.G.4	6.EE.4

Student Names

—see analysis for constructed response

Notes

Notes

Notes

Notes

Notes

Notes